NO FORGIVENESS

HISTORY OF INDIA'S FREEDOM STRUGGLE

PRAKASH ROY

Contents

No Forgiveness
by Prakash Roy
	1ˢᵗ Publicat
	ion: November 2021
2ⁿᵈ Publication: January 2024
	Publication: March 2025
Author: Prakash Roy

Cover: Prakash Roy
Typesetting: Prakash Roy

Publisher: Notion Press, Inc.
800, West EI Camino Real #180,
California USA 94040
	Notion Press Media Pvt Ltd,
#7, Red Cross Road,
Egmore, Chennai, Tamil Nadu 600008

I am Prakash Roy,
with the blessings of my parents,
I dedicate this book to the revolutionary Kanailal Dutt...

About The Book

We were subjugated for almost two hundred years, But this India did not get freedom like this. After the assassination of Siraj-ud-Daula, the British Empire snatched India's independence. Gradually they conquered almost the whole of India. Sirajuddaula was defeated only because of Mir Jafar. Similarly, the reason why this country remained subjugated for two hundred years was because of the birth of a thousand Mir Jafars. After the arrival of the Age of Fire, the various plans of the revolutionaries began. The oppression of the British began. The revolutionaries were dissatisfied with the actions of the treacherous traitors. Traitor Nandalal Banerjee handed over Prafulla Chaki, Naren Gonsai betrayed in Alipore bomb case. The injustice done to the revolutionaries by government lawyers Ashutosh Biswas and Shamshul Alam was not tolerated in the revolutionary circles. Therefore, killing traitors first became the main objective of the revolutionaries. At the same time, the revolutionaries noticed the oppressive British officers as well. So this book highlights the murders of traitorous, traitorous and tyrannical British officers. The revolutionaries were successful in the murders. Thousands of young men lost their lives in the struggle to liberate this motherland. From Bengal to the whole of India, the revolutionaries' rampage of the new sunrise began. Through this book, an attempt has been made to bring out the stories of those heroes who have been lost in oblivion. In whose sacrifice we see the sunrise of freedom. The book is titled "No Forgiveness" about the murder of tyrannical British officers, traitors and traitors. We need to inform the new generation about the history of the bloody freedom struggle. I extend my love to all my dear readers. I invite everyone to read the book. I hope you will enjoy reading the book. "Vande Mataram."

Prakash Roy

About The Author

Since childhood, he had a dream that he would work for the country. So he wanted to join the army. From the age of about 6-7, he wanted to know about the biographies of the country's brave warriors and freedom fighters. Our author's name is Prakash Roy. He was born on March 14, 1996 in Satvendi village of Jalpaiguri district of West Bengal. He received his first education at Panbari Barmanpara RR School, after which he joined Panbari Bhabani High School.

He tried to study a lot while fighting against family hardships, but he had to admit defeat in front of family hardships. His dream did not come true, his dream remained. Gradually, he started telling the people of the country through social media who had sacrificed for the country. We do not know about all the patriots, so he tries to present the stories of all the patriots to everyone.

Gradually, he won the hearts of many on social media and, as per the readers' wishes, he started writing books. He started writing his books and named his first Bengali book 'Kshama Nei Deshdrohi'.

Book References

Bengali Books

1. Bharate Sashastra Biplab - Bhupendrakumar Rakshit Roy
2. Chattogram Yuba Bidroha - Ananta Singha
3. Muktir Sangrame Bharat - West Bengal Bangla Academy
4. Bharater Boiplabik Sangramer Itihas- Suprakash Roy
5. Bharater Swadhinata Sangramer Sangkhipta Itihas - Upendra chandra Bhattacharya
6. Bir Biplabi Bhagat Singh - Prithviraj Sen
7. Nirbachita Biplabider Chelebela - Prithviraj Sen
8. Ami Subhas Bolchi - Shailesh Dey
9. Bharatborsher Swadhinata Juddher Itihas - Sukumar Roy
10. Khudiram o Prafulla Chaki - Gopal Bhowmik
11. Bagha Jatin - Mani Bagchi
12. Sangsad Bengali Charitavidhan

Hindi Books

1. Krantikari Kosh - Saral Krishna
2. Swatatrata Senani Granthmala - Phulchand Jain
3. Bhagat Singh or Unka Jug - Manmathanath Gupta
4. Bhagat Singh or Unka Sathiyoke Dastabhej - Jagmohan Singh
5. Azadi Ke Deewana - Rajendrakumar Tandon
6. Bharatiya Charitakosh

The murder of Mr. Rand and Lieutenant Ayerst And the murder of the traitors Ganesh Shankar and Ramachandra

Even today, the sacrifice of three brothers (Bhai) is remembered with reverence in Chinchwad village of Pune district of Maharashtra. They were born in a noble Brahmin family. One by one, the three brothers sang the song of victory of life on the gallows. Such sacrifice of three brothers is rare in history.

The time was 1896-97, at that time, a great darkness descended on Maharashtra. The cries of the people spread everywhere, on one hand due to the oppression of the British and on the other hand, a danger called plague came. Gradually, this plague spread throughout the country and took the form of a epidemic. The British government could not find a way to suppress this epidemic, and in the end, the British rulers failed and passed a new law. They passed such a law that people feared the British government more than the plague epidemic. This law was named the 'Epidemic

Disease Act', which means epidemic suppression. With the help of this law, government officials could enter anyone's house and conduct tests if they sensed anything suspicious. This law was absolutely necessary in the case of contagious diseases. But the purpose of the officials was more different in the eyes of the people.

The British carried out brutal atrocities in the name of this plague epidemic, and Mr. Rand was the king of this atrocities. The atrocities increased to such an extent that women's bodies were stripped naked for physical examination. Suspects were tortured on the streets and at the ghats, and ordinary and innocent people finally started fleeing the villages and cities due to fear of shame and torture. Balgangadhar Tilak strongly protested against this and expressed his opposition through his writing 'Dainik Keshari'. Those heroes, whose eyes were burning with the fire of rebellion in their protest language, did not flee from the villages and cities. They knew that if we also fled, then to whom would the common people look. One day, what will history say, that is why they did not flee and stood firm. When the country is ours, why should we leave our homes and this village?

This time, no matter what, the British tyrants will have to be driven out of this country. A great leader like Balgangadhar Tilak came forward, and his revolutionary mantra inspired three brothers named 'Chapekar Bandhu': Damodar Hari Chapekar, Balkrishna Hari Chapekar, Vasudev Hari Chapekar, Mahadev Vinayak Ranade and Khande Rao Sathe. Now, a plan to kill Mr. Rand began to be discussed among the revolutionaries. And the names of Damodar Hari Chapekar, Balkrishna Hari Chapekar and Mahadev Vinayak Ranade came up in this campaign. As planned, the 60th "Jubilee" of Queen Victoria is being celebrated all over the country at Government House. And Mr. Rand will be present there, The revolutionaries will attack him on his way back from the ceremony.

The day of waiting slowly came, the day was June 22, 1897. Damodar Hari Chapekar and his brother Balkrishna Chapekar and the other one was Mahadev Vinayak Ranade. They were waiting for this opportunity. Government House was located in the

Ganeshkhind area of Poona city. The "Jubilee" ceremony was being celebrated there. Big British officials went there and made a lot of noise. The revolutionaries were also around Government House. That day, they could not attack Rand even after getting close to him repeatedly. Still, they held their patience tightly, not now, they will wait for an hour or two, not for months or years. After that, Damodar, Balkrishna and Vinayak decided to kill Rand on the way back from the ceremony. They started waiting for Rand to return.

Rand and Ayerst left the Government House at around 11:30 PM. Damodar was hiding a little away from the function hall, and Balakrishna a little further away, and Vinayak Ranade was waiting a little further away. Now Ayerst and his wife came out in a horse-drawn carriage, followed by Rand. As soon as the carriage drew near, Damodar jumped up behind Rand's carriage, and it wasn't long before Damodar's pistol roared. Rand fell down there. What happened next? Ayerst and his wife were shocked to hear the roar of the pistol. In a flash, Vinayak Ranadc jumped on Ayerst with a pistol and his pistol also roared in the same way. Ayerst immediately collapsed in his wife's lap. The work of the three revolutionaries was successful, so without further delay, they disappeared into the darkness of the night. They left no evidence behind.

No one could figure out who had orchestrated the murder. After that, the revolutionaries were roaming around freely, while the British government could not find any evidence. What did the British government do now? They hired spies. They hired Ganesh Shankar Dravid and Ramchandra Dravid as spies and is two brothers. These were famous criminals, it was difficult for the British to find skilled anti-social people like them. The British told them that if the two brothers could provide any evidence and identify the killers, they could be released from jail. They would also be rewarded with twenty thousand taka. They agreed to do this work out of greed for money.

Ramachandra Dravid was especially after Vasudev and Vinayak Ranad, due to which they were repeatedly called to the police station for qucstioning and various questions were asked. Thus, with the help of Ganesh Shankar Dravid and Ramachandra Dravid, Damodar Hari Chapekar was arrested on August 9. The trial began, the court sentenced Damodar Hari Chapekar to death. Then Damodar asked: That's it! Nothing more?... The day of execution was set for April 18, 1898. The heroic revolutionary Damodar Hari Chapekar stood on the gallows with the Bhagavad Gita in his hand.

Finally, in 1898, due to betrayal of trust, Balkrishna Hari Chapekar was caught in Hyderabad. The name of the person who had betrayed Balkrishna Chapekar was Head Constable Rampandu. On 10th February 1899, a case was filed against Balkrishna Chapekar in the court of the Pune City Magistrate. In this case, Balkrishna Chapekar was sentenced to death. Vasudev Chapekar came to meet him. He was not only Balkrishna Chapekar's brother, he was the apple of his eye. The British were so cruel that they did not allow the two brothers to meet. Balkrishna Chapekar was just waiting for the time when the noose would fall around his neck with a smile on his face.

Vasudev and Mahadev Vinayak Ranade are doing the work of revolution well, the fire of rebellion is burning in Vasudev's mind. The two brothers are in jail for some betrayal. Vasudev thought that as long as these traitors are alive, they will expose the stories of various revolutionaries. Then their condition will also be like Damodar and Balakrishna, first these traitors will have to bid farewell to this world forever. This time, he will kill the traitors with his own hands. The first target of their conspiracy is Constable Rampandu. The day was 3rd February 1899, the two revolutionaries Vasudev and Vinayak Ranade went out, but they did not get the proper facilities that day. So they could not succeed that day. Then 8th February 1899, the two revolutionaries Vasudev and Vinayak Ranade were hiding on the side of the road in the dark night. They were waiting for Constable Rampandu, he would be killed on his way home. That day too, their wait failed.

That day another idea came to their mind, today Rampandu did not come but two more traitors are still alive. Today they have to be noticed. The names of these two traitors are Ganeshshankar

Drabid and Ramchandra Drabid, these two brothers had betrayed Damodar for the greed of twenty thousand rupees. Vasudev and Vinayak Ranade together set off to the house of Ganeshshankar Drabid and Ramchandra Drabid. Ganeshshankar and Ramchandra were at home that day. That day the two brothers were playing cards together. Because of them, Vinayak and Basudev had to go to the police station repeatedly, where they were asked various questions. They were tricked into calling them out of their homes. They were told that the Superintendent of Police had called them to the police station for a special reason. Meanwhile, Vasudev, Vinayak Ranade and revolutionary Khande Rao Sathe were waiting outside with pistols in hand. It didn't take long for Ganesh Shankar and Ramachandra to come out, as soon as they came out, the pistols of the three revolutionaries roared.

Ganeshshankar Drabid and Ramchandra Drabid fell to the ground immediately after being hit by the bullets, Ganeshshankar Drabid died on the spot and his brother Ramchandra Drabid was seriously injured and was admitted to the hospital. Immediately, the three revolutionaries disappeared into the darkness of the night, a crowd of people gathered around them, and the two traitors were lying on the ground. No one could even guess who had committed this gruesome murder. The arrival of the British forces was of no avail. The police's suspicions on Basudev increased, and they were keeping an eye on their friends. Now the police station was called, and Basudev, Vinayak Ranade and Khande Rao Sathe appeared at the police station. Before going to the police station, they took a pistol with them in case Rampandu was found there. But the police were alert that day, they were first searched before entering the police station, and after the search, firearms were found in their possession. Then they were immediately arrested. They themselves announced that they had killed the traitors, because there is no place for traitors in our country.

One by one, all four were martyred on the same gallows in the "Jarbeda" jail. Damodar Chapekar was hanged earlier on 18 April 1899. Then on 8 May 1899, Vasudev Hari Chapekar, then came Vinayak's turn on 10 May 1899. Finally, on 12 May 1899, Balkrishna Chapekar was also hanged. This was the life story of the four revolutionaries. They were hanging by the noose while laughing for the country. And in the revolutionary khonde Rao Sathe was given ten years of rigorous imprisonment.

Damodar Hari Chapekar

Damodar Chapekar was born in Chinchwad village in Pune district of Maharashtra. His father was a famous prayer singer- Haripant Chapekar. Damodar Hari Chapekar wanted to become a soldier since childhood, but being a Brahmin, the British did not accept him as a soldier. He inherited the fame of Kirtan. Lokmanya Bal Gangadhar Tilak was Damodar Hari Chapekar's idol.

"Chapekar's friend" Damodar Hari Chapekar, Balkrishna Chapekar and Vasudev Chapekar considered Lokmanya Bal Gangadhar Tilak as their guru. In the year 1897, the city of Pune was suffering from a terrible epidemic like plague. On this occasion, the British government committed unspeakable atrocities on the people of India. Mr. Rand was one of the British oppressors. Damodar Hari Chapekar killed this Rand.

Damodar Hari Chapekar was arrested because of the traitor Ganesh Shankar Dravid and his brother Ramchandra Dravid. He was sentenced to death in the trial. He died on the gallows in the "Jarbeda" jail on 18 April 1898.

Balkrishna Hari Chapekar

Balkrishna Hari Chapekar was born in 1873 in a Brahmin family in Chitpavan, Maharashtra. His father's name was Haripant Chapekar, he used to do kirtan. Haripant Chapekar used to go to different places and recite kirtan and mythological stories and run his family with this.

In the year 1897, the city of Pune was suffering from a terrible epidemic like plague. On this occasion, the British government took the opportunity to commit unspeakable atrocities on the people of India. Mr. Rand was one of the British tyrants. In any case, this tyrant had to be killed, the day was June 22, 1897, which was the 60th "Jubilee" of Queen Victoria at Government House, which was being celebrated all over the country.

There, Damodar Hari Chapekar and Balkrishna Hari Chapekar killed Rand and Ayerst.

With the help of Constable Rampandu, the British government was able to arrest Balkrishna Chapekar in 1898. On 10 February 1899, a case was filed against Balkrishna Chapekar in the court of the Poona City Magistrate. In this case, Balkrishna Chapekar was sentenced to death. On 12 May 1899, Balkrishna Chapekar was hanged in the "Jarbeda" jail.

Vasudev Hari Chapekar

Vasudev Hari Chapekar was born in 1880. His father's name was Haripant Chapekar. Vasudev Chapekar's education began in the Marathi language of Maharashtra. Over time, the three brothers would travel around to help their father by singing kirtans. What if Vasudev was much younger, his work was unparalleled.

On June 22, 1897, Queen Victoria's 60th "Jubilee" was celebrated at Government House, which was being celebrated all over the country. It was there that Rand and Ayerst were killed by Damodar Hari Chapekar and Balkrishna Hari Chapekar.

Damodar Hari Chapekar was arrested because of the traitor Ganesh Shankar Dravid and his brother Ramchandra Dravid. With the help of Constable Rampandu, the British government was able to arrest Balkrishna Chapekar in 1898. He was sentenced to death by the trial court for the murder of the traitor Ganesh Shankar Dravid and his brother Ramchandra Dravid. On 8 May 1899, Vasudev Hari Chapekar was hanged in the "Jarbeda" jail.

Mahadev Vinayak Ranade

Mahadev Vinayak Ranade was born in Pune, Maharashtra. His father's name was Vinayak Ranade. In 1897, he and Chapekar's two brothers Damodar Hari Chapekar and Balkrishna Hari Chapekar killed the 'Plague' Commissioner Mr. Rand and Lieutenant Ayerst.

In this murder, Damodar Hari Chapekar was arrested due to the With the help of two royal witnesses and the traitor Ganesh Shankar Dravid and his brother Ramchandra Dravid. With the help of Constable Rampandu, the British government was able to arrest Balkrishna Chapekar. Mahadev Vinayak Ranade was sentenced to death for the murder of the traitor Ganesh Shankar Dravid and his brother Ramchandra Dravid.

Mahadev Vinayak Ranade was hanged in the "Jarbeda" jail on 10 May 1899.

Khande Rao Sathe

Damodar Hari Chapekar and Balkrishna Hari Chapekar killed the 'Plague' Commissioner Mr. Rand and Lieutenant Ayerst.

Damodar Hari Chapekar was arrested because of the two royal witnesses and the traitor Ganesh Shankar Dravid and his brother Ramchandra Dravid in this murder. With the help of Constable Rampandu, the British government was able to arrest Balkrishna Chapekar. He killed the traitor Ganesh Shankar Dravid and his brother Ramchandra Dravid.

A few days later, Khande Rao Sathe, Mahadev Vinayak Ranade and Vasudev were arrested by the police. Mahadev Vinayak Ranade and Vasudev were sentenced to death in the trial. Revolutionary Khande Rao Sathe was sentenced to ten years of rigorous imprisonment due to his young age.

CHAPTER TWO

Inspector Nandalal Banerjee Murder

On 30th April 1908, Khudiram Bose and Prafulla Chaki threw a bomb at the car of the District Magistrate, the tyrannical British officer Kingsford. Unfortunately, Kingsford was not in the car that day. So, by mistake, Mrs. Kennedy and her daughter lost their lives in their bomb throw. Within a moment, the news spread everywhere. As soon as the bomb was thrown, they started running away. After going some distance, they took two separate paths as they had planned.

Even after all this, Prafulla and Khudiram did not know their real identities. Khudiram Bose knew that Prafulla Chaki was Dinesh Roy and Prafulla Chaki knew that Khudiram was Haren Sarkar. Then the two ran in different directions. Khudiram Bose was caught after reaching Waini station. On the other hand, Prafulla Chaki ran for about 40 miles towards Samastipur station. Samastipur station was a little further away, and Prafulla wanted to go there. Suddenly, an unknown gentleman came and stopped him from going to the station. He said, "Come with me, I will drop you off on time." This raised a suspicion in Prafulla Chaki's mind. How could he trust an unknown gentleman? Prafulla touched the pistol in his pocket. It was better to be careful.

Even though the stranger didn't say anything, he understood Prafulla Chaki's true identity. Prafulla was barefoot, with dust and dirt on his clothes. If he went to the station in this condition, the police would recognize him in a moment. So the stranger brought Prafulla new clothes and shoes. After staying with him all day, he wished Prafulla well and said goodbye.

Prafulla Chaki bought a ticket for Mokamaghat and sat down in a corner of the platform. At that moment, Sub-Inspector Nandalal Banerjee arrived on the platform. He had just from vacation and was returning to work. How did Prafulla Chaki attract attention? New clothes, new shoes. A little doubt arose in Nandalal's mind. Meanwhile, Prafulla is lost in thought about how Khudiram is doing. Meanwhile, Nandalal Banerjee tries to connect with Prafulla.

Prafulla approaches the and expresses his sympathy for the Nandalal revolutionaries. Meanwhile, Prafulla is lost in thought, not wanting to talk to Nandalal, but still having to talk to him. He is a skilled police officer, He knows very well how to find out secrets. Nandalal came closer and said, "A bomb was thrown at Mr. Kennedy's car early in the morning, killing Mrs. Kennedy and her daughter." Hearing this, Prafulla was suddenly shocked, wondering what we had done. We had killed two innocent women, our long-planned plan had finally failed. That meant Kingsford was not dead.

But this thought of Prafulla Chaki could not escape Nandalal's eyes. Nandalal realized that this was the fugitive, and his greedy heart danced with joy. If he could hand him over, he would receive a large sum of money as a reward. Meanwhile, Nandalal wired the nearest police station in Muzaffarpur, and Nandalal immediately received an order to arrest him. Prafulla also got annoyed by Nandalal's behavior. As soon as the train arrived, Prafulla went to a compartment of the train and sat down. Nandalal also went to the same compartment and sat down. Meanwhile, the armed police force was ready at Mokamaghat.

As soon as Prafulla got off the train, Nandalal went to arrest him. Prafulla said: 'Shit, you are a Bengali and are betraying another Bengali? Is this your job?' Prafulla had infinite strength in his body, he freed himself from the police in a flash and started running. Two constables stopped him and stood at one end of the platform. That day was May 1, 1908, when the clock had struck 6 o'clock. Prafulla finally aimed the barrel of his pistol at his own forehead and fired a shot, his lifeless body falling to the ground at the station.

Prafulla told Nandalal that his real name was Dinesh Chandra Roy. Then his body was sent to Khudiram. Khudiram recognized him immediately. Even then, the British government did a great job, separated Prafulla Chaki's head from his body and sent it to Calcutta. Nandalal was also promoted in his job.

Six months and eight days passed, the day was November 9, 1908. Revolutionary Shrish Chandra Pal (alias Naren) and the fierce revolutionary Ranen Ganguly (alias Ranendranath) went out together towards the house of traitor Nandalal Banerjee. They were waiting for Nandalal to come out of his house. By then, the clock had struck exactly 7 o'clock. Nandalal was seen coming out of his house. Now Ranen Ganguly and Shrish Chandra Pal followed him. Nandalal was walking along the Serpentine Lane with some papers. Suddenly, a voice was heard from behind - 'Stop.' Nandalal looked back and saw two unknown young men. Nandalal said - 'What do you want'? The reply came in the form of 'I want to reward you.' In an instant, the revolutionaries' pistols roared three times, and Nandalal Banerjee's body was lying on the road.

To reassure himself, Ranen Ganguly started hitting the dead Nandalal on the head with the pistol again. Nandalal was dead and unharmed, so without wasting much time, he disappeared from the scene in an instant. No one could even find out who had done this. Not to mention the police, many revolutionaries did not even know about this.

Prafulla Chaki

Prafulla Chaki was born on December 10, 1888 in Rangpur. Their original residence was Bogra Bihar village. His father's name was Rajnarayan Chaki. Prafulla studied at Rangpur School, where he built a wrestling arena. He would spend his days wrestling with his peers. Apart from wrestling, he also mastered stick fighting, knife fighting and sword fighting. At a very young age, he became a member of the National Secret Center.

Prafulla joined the Bandhav Samiti while he was a school student. During the national movement, a national school was established in Rangpur. Prafulla was given a huge responsibility. He had to teach young students how to play the stick and fight. The students got a proper education through his teachings. Then he also formed a relief committee to fight any adversities. He used to feed the common people.

In 1906, Prafulla Chaki went to Kolkata with Barin Ghosh (alias Barindrakumar Ghosh). Then he planned to kill the tyrant of East Bengal, Chotolat Bamfilt Fuller, under the leadership of Barin Ghosh. When this plan failed, he went to Maniktala. There he took refuge in a garden house at 32 Muraripukur Lane. Then the revolutionaries decided to kill the tyrant Presidency Magistrate Kingsford of Kolkata.

Seeing the spirit of the revolutionaries, the British government transferred Kingsford to Muzaffarpur. Then, as planned, two people were sent to Muzaffarpur. They were none other than Prafulla Chaki and Khudiram Bose. These two young men went to Muzaffarpur and stayed in a hospice. They spent a few days there, during which they gathered all the information about Kingsford. When and where was Kingsford going, from where and when was he returning.

This time Prafulla Chaki and Khudiram Bose set out on the adventurous mission of killing Kingsford. The day was April 30, 1908. The clock struck 8:30, and Prafulla Chaki and Khudiram Bose were waiting outside the European Club. Seeing Kingsford's Fitton car leaving the club, the two revolutionaries exchanged glances. Immediately, an explosion was heard. Both of them smiled, they had succeeded. But unfortunately, Kingsford was not in the car that day. As a result, Mrs. Kennedy and her daughter died.

Immediately after the explosion, Prafulla Chaki and Khudiram Basu disappeared in both directions. Prafulla Chaki ran towards Samastipur on foot all night. Before Samastipur station, a gentleman helped Prafulla a lot. He brought new clothes and shoes and gave him shelter in his house for the whole day. Then Prafulla bought a ticket for Samastipur station Mokamaghat and boarded the train. After getting down at Mokamaghat, Nandalal Banerjee tried to arrest Prafulla with the help of some constables.

What did Prafulla Chaki do, instead of being captured by the British government, he took out his pistol and sacrificed himself. The pseudonym of this revolutionary of the Age of Fire was Dinesh Chandra Roy. Another name that needs to be mentioned here is that a gentleman who helps Prafulla before Samastipur station is the patriot Trigunacharan Ghosh. If he had not helped Prafulla Chaki that day, Prafulla Chaki might have been caught long ago.

Shrishchandra Pal

Shrishchandra Pal was born in approximately 1887 in Malibagh, Dhaka. In 1905, he was introduced to the secret revolutionary party. He joined Hemchandra Ghosh's revolutionary party Mukti Sangha and later the Bengal Volunteers. Shrishchandra Pal was one of the revolutionary soldiers in the adventurous activities of the revolutionary party. But he was one of the devotees of Netaji Subhas Chandra Bose. In 1908, Nandalal Banerjee betrayed the revolutionary Prafulla Chaki, who was involved in the Kingsford assassination conspiracy. Prafulla Chaki died a heroic death because of his betrayal.

This time, if the traitor police inspector Nandalal Banerjee cannot be finished, the revolution will not sleep. Then the revolutionaries decide to kill Nandalal Banerjee as planned. Srish Pal's main task is to kill Nandalal Banerjee. Because he has to avenge the death of Prafulla Chaki. If there is a traitor like Nandalal in this country, the revolution will never succeed. If Nandalal is alive, he will expose many more revolutionaries in the future.

Srish Pal would play the main role in the murder of Nandalal, and the responsibility of this work fell to another young revolutionary. On the evening of November 9, 1908, they shot Nandalal dead in Serpentine Lane, Kolkata. Despite a lot of searching, the police could not find any evidence.

In 1912, the revolutionaries were plotting to kill the tyrant O'Brien. On the advice of Shrish Pal and Anukulbabu of Atmonnati, Haridas Dutta and Khagen Das (alias Khagendranath Das) went to work as coolies in the company of the tyrant engineer Robert O'Brien of the Alexander Jute Mills in the Jagaddal area. They kept an eye on Robert O'Brien day after day for three months. In the end, their plan was exposed and they failed. After that, Shrish Pal, Khagen Das and Haridas Mitra had to hide for a long time. Nevertheless, Shrish Pal kept in touch with the revolutionary party in disguise.

Then Srish Pal participated in the famous Roda Company arms theft operation. On 26 August 1914, a box of Mauser pistols from Roda Company was stolen in broad daylight on the highway under the leadership of revolutionary Srish Chandra Mitra (alias Habu Mitra).

Srish Chandra Pal and Haridas Dutta set out to bring the weapons in the guise of a bullock cart driver. Like other vehicles, the boxes of weapons were also loaded into Srish Pal's vehicle. He cleverly took the car loaded with weapons to the revolutionary center by throwing dust in the eyes of the police. He was helped in this task by Khagen Das (alias Khagendranath Das), a revolutionary of the Mukti Sangh.

Finally, he was arrested in 1916. After that, he was imprisoned for a long time. Srish Pal was released in 1919 due to illness. The revolutionary Srish Chandra Pal breathed his last in 1939.

Bipin Bihari Ganguly

The murderer of Nandalal Banerjee was none other than Ranen Ganguly, Ranen Ganguly was a pseudonym. On November 9, 1908, Shrish Pal and Ranen Ganguly shot and killed Nandalal in the evening at Serpentine Lane in Kolkata. Despite a lot of searching, the police could not find any evidence. This Ranen Ganguly is Bipin Bihari Ganguly. He was born on November 5, 1887. Bipin

Ganguly's original residence was in Halishahar, North 24 Parganas district. His father's name was Akshaynath Ganguly. Bipin Ganguly not only killed Nandalal Banerjee, he was also specially involved in the kidnapping of arms from the Roda Company.

Bipin Ganguly was inspired by the revolutionary mantra after coming in contact with Mahanayak Rash Behari Bose and Barindra Kumar Ghosh. He had contacts with various revolutionary groups. He was a member of Jugantar Dal and Atmonnati Samiti. Atmonnati Samiti was established in 1897 and accepted his membership. Then in 1914, he kidnapped the Mauser pistol of Roda Company. This kidnapping was carried out as per Bipin Ganguly's plan. After the kidnapping, all those firearms were sent to various centers of revolutionaries. So that everyone could use these firearms for revolutionary work.

Bipin Ganguly's story does not end here, he has done several important works. He also worked with the heroic revolutionary Jatindranath. In 1915, as per the plan of the Jugantar Party, he kidnapped the Bird Company's car as an assistant of Jatindranath (Bagha Jatin). After some time, Bipin Ganguly joined the Congress movement in 1921.

Bipin Ganguly presided over the Bengal Provincial Congress Conference in 1930. Then again after some time, he joined the 'Quit India' movement. He spent 28 years in various jails while in prison. Finally, this great revolutionary passed away on 14th January 1954.

CHAPTER THREE

Traitor Naren Gosai Murder Case

It was the time of India's freedom struggle, just as revolutionaries sacrificed their lives with a smile on their faces, some traitors were also born. The year was 1908, the revolution had become desperate.

The country's independence must be wrested from the British, or else we will die or be killed. And those who, as citizens of India, commit treason against the noble sons of Mother India, will be executed by the revolutionaries.

'Alipur Conspiracy Case' which is also known as Alipur Bomb Case. Many revolutionaries of Bengal are imprisoned in this conspiracy case. The revolutionaries who were arrested in the Alipur Bomb Case were - Sri Aurobindo Ghosh, Barindra Kumar Ghosh (Barin Ghosh), Upendranath Banerjee, Bibhuti Bhushan Sarkar, Abinash Chandra Bhattacharya, Ullaskar Dutta, Ashok Kumar Nandi, Narendra Goswami (Naren Gosai), Satyendranath Bose and Kanailal Dutta and many others. A case was filed against them in the court, and a farce was carried out in the name of trial. At that time, Narendra Goswami i.e. Naren Gosai became the prime witness in the same case. The young revolutionaries were unhappy with his behavior. Now, talks started among the revolutionaries, no matter what, Naren Gosai will have to pay the price for this. After discussion, it was confirmed that death by betrayal was the only way out.

Now, to kill Naren Gosai, we need a pistol, how can we get one pistol while sitting in jail? Hemchandra Das Kanungo proposed that if the two pistols of the European Warder were snatched away, Ullasakar Dutta did not agree to this proposal, saying that it would be even more dangerous. Then Kanailal Dutta and Satyendranath Bose (Satyan Bose) said that if they could collect two pistols for us, then we would kill Naren Gosai no matter what. Then Hemchandra Das Kanungo collected two pistols from outside and brought them to the two.

Since Naren Gosai was a royal witness, the police were teaching him what to say in court. His danger was inevitable for his royal witness, so he was kept in the first degree. But it would not work if had a pistol in his hand, the one I would kill would have to be within reach. He was imprisoned in another cell. No matter what, he would have to be brought face to face. Now Kanai and Satyen (Kanailal Dutta and Satyendranath Bose) hatched a conspiracy. Then Satyen Bose feigned illness and was admitted to the jail hospital on 27th July 1908. Kanailal was admitted to the same hospital on 30th August feigning illness. Their conspiracy was about to succeed, this time Satyen Bose wrote a letter to Naren Gosai saying that he was very ill. I also want to live, so I want to be a royal witness.

Naren Gosai was overjoyed, he had found a partner to be a witness. Satyen Basu also said that I want to talk to you directly about this matter, I am admitted in the jail and hospital. Naren Gosai spoke to the district magistrate and took permission. Satyen spoke to Naren on August 29th, and it was agreed that they would talk about this matter again the next morning, that is, on August 30th.

Now it was just a matter of waiting, the time was slowly approaching. The day was September 1, 1908, Naren Gosai came to meet Satyen. Naren Gosai brought Higgins, the European warder, with him. Naren Gosai was sitting in the dispensary, because the discussion was confidential. Satyen Bose was called, then Satyen Bose also came there. Before the conversation could begin between them, Satyen's pistol roared, and Naren Gosai was shot of the moment. Naren, shot, started running to Higgins' shelter, and

Higgins was shot in a moment. Higgins and Naren Gosai ran to save their lives, Naren ran out of the hospital. Satyen Bose and Kanailal Dutta followed them.

The bullets were raining down from Kanailal Dutta's pistol. Suddenly, a man named Linton grabbed Kanai. Kanailal Dutta's pistol had only one bullet left, so Kanai hit Linton on the head with that pistol without wasting the bullet. Finally, Kanailal's last bullet also roared out of his hand, Naren Gosai fell into a drain. Then the two revolutionaries were caught by the police. Seeing this horrific murder, the British Empire trembled.

Then, what started was the trial. This case went from the court to the High Court, the day was October 21, 1908. As usual, the two revolutionaries, Kanailal Dutta and Satyendranath Bose, were sentenced to death in the trial. When Kanailal was presented in court, he said one thing, "I have nothing to say, I know what my sentence will be. I killed the traitor Naren Gosai, Satyendranath is not guilty, let him go. Just tell me when I will be hanged."

Kanailal Dutta died on the gallows in Alipore Central Jail on November 10, 1908. Satyendranath Bose was also hanged on November 21.

Kanailal Dutta

Kanailal Dutta was born on 31 August 1888 in Chandannagar. His father's name was Chunilal Dutta. Kanai's childhood was spent in Bombay. Later he returned to Chandannagar. There he received his education from Duplex Vidyamandir and later from Mohsin College in Hooghly district. Then he met the great revolutionary Charuchandra Roy. Charuchandra Roy was the director of the revolutionary magazine 'Jugantar'. Kanailal was initiated into the revolutionary mantra by Charuchandra Roy. Then he passed the B.A. examination and joined the active revolutionary party in Calcutta.

He established close contact with the revolutionary party in Calcutta. He participated in various meetings and events of the revolutionaries. Within a few days, Kanai became a trusted friend of the revolutionaries. The important work of the revolutionaries was entrusted to him. He would stay up all night writing leaflets. The next morning, he would distribute those leaflets to various revolutionary centers. He knew that there were many risks in this work, but he was not afraid of anyone.

On 2nd May 1908, Kanai was arrested in the 'Muraripukur Bomb Case' of Lane No. 32. He was kept in Alipore Central Jail during the trial. At that time, a revolutionary friend of his asked him to become a royal witness. His name was Narendranath Goswami, i.e. Naren Gosai. Then Kanai Lal Dutt and Satyendranath Bose planned to kill the traitor Naren Gosai and they succeeded in that plan. What courage, what an impossible task they made possible from jail.

Kanai was brought to court in the garb of a prisoner. He did not call any lawyer for himself. In the court, he clearly said, "I killed Naren Gosai, Satyen (Satyendranath Bose) was not present at the scene. He is not guilty, I killed him alone." The judge asked him, "Where did you get the pistol?" Kanailal smiled and replied, "I got the pistol from the soul of Khudiram Basu."

Kanai was sentenced to death in the trial, and the High Court upheld his death sentence. An unusual thing happened while Kanai was in jail, Kanai gained 16 pounds. Finally, on November 10, 1908, the clock struck seven. Kanai stood on the death platform and happily took the noose around his neck. Some time before the execution, Kanai's mother came to visit her son in jail. Then what did Kanai say to her mother - 'You were only my mother until now, look, today you have become the mother of the whole country.'

On the day of the execution, a surprising incident occurred, thousands of people outside the jail were desperate to see his body. When the body was brought out, people from all castes, regardless of their caste, were showering flowers on it. It was a tearful scene. The flowers that fell on the ground were touched on their foreheads by all the countrymen that day. The countrymen were watching their nation's red being burnt to ashes in the blazing flames.

Satyendranath Bose

Satyendranath Bose was born on 30 July 1882 in Medinipur. His father's name was Abhaycharan Bose. Satyendranath Bose passed the entrance exam from the Collegiate School in 1897. In 1899, he was admitted to the City College to study B.A. Due to physical weakness, he did not get the opportunity to take the B.A. examination.

Satyendranath Bose became involved in revolutionary activities from 1902. Then in 1906, Hemchandra Das Kanungo went to Paris to learn the techniques of bomb making, that is, to learn how to make bombs. For this, Satyendranath Bose was appointed as the district organizer in place of Hemchandra Das Kanungo. In 1908, he was arrested for possessing a gun. He was a prisoner in the Medinipur jail under trial. After that, he was accused of the famous 'Alipur Bomb Case' and taken to Calcutta. During the trial, a man named Naren Gosai betrayed him. He decided to kill Naren Gosai inside the jail. He was accompanied by Kanailal Dutta. The main conspirators were Hemchandra Das Kanungo and Ullaskar Dutta.

On September 1, 1908, Satyendranath Bose and Kanailal Dutta shot and killed Naren Gosai. The trial sentenced both to death.

Satyendranath Bose was hanged on November 21, 1908. That day, hundreds of people gathered outside the jail to take the dead body of the hero. But the British government was so cruel that they issued a new law. According to them, no body would be given to the relatives of the accused. If the body was taken outside, the public would start rioting. So Satyendranath Bose's body was burned in the jail's crematorium.

Hundreds of people waited, they did not see the dead body of their hero. Finally, they had to return.

CHAPTER FOUR

Government Lawyer Ashutosh Biswas Murder

When a citizen of this country files a false case against the youth of this country in court, who will hunt down this lie? Yes, there was such a man, his name was Ashutosh Biswas, he was called Ashu in court. He was a public prosecutor, that is, a government lawyer. His name is very famous to the British, in a word, he is an agent of the British government. Framing a false case is not a difficult task for him. He knows very well how to frame false cases against homegrown revolutionaries and Government witnesses must be prepared.

Such behavior was not tolerated in the revolutionary circle. First, Nandalal Banerjee was killed, then the traitor Naren Gosai. After that, the order came, remove the traitor Ashutosh Biswas. Such a seal was placed on the revolutionary circle of the Anushila Samiti. But who will participate in this campaign? Who will be the rightful owner. A young rival came forward. He may be crippled, weak and short, but there is a burning flame hidden inside him. His name is Charuchandra Bose. Charu Bose's right hand is completely immobile, he has been a rival since birth. The leaves and fingers of his right hand are missing from birth.

Despite being a rival, who knew that he had a touch of fire in his heart. It is known that Jatindranath Mukherjee (Bagha Jatin) himself inspired the revolution in his heart. Charu Bose lived in house number 1/1, Kedar Bose Lane. That house belonged to revolutionary Gishpati Roy Chowdhury. Then from there he would go to work at No. 136-B 'Hitashi Press' which is located on Rosa Road.

Charuchandra Bose now had to reach his goal. The day was February 10, 1909, Charuchandra set out to kill Ashutosh with a vow to fulfill his duty. He tied a pistol tightly in his right hand, and with his left hand he would pull the trigger to kill the enemy. Charu arrived at Alipore Court, and spent the whole day waiting for Ashu. Towards the afternoon, Ashu was seen coming out of the court, Charu reached on time and blocked Ashu's way. Charu extended her crippled hand in front of Ashu, and before Ashu could understand anything, Charu pulled the trigger of the pistol with his left hand. Charu's pistol roared with a loud noise.

Ashutosh Biswas's body lay in front of the Alipore court. Another traitor got the death sentence at the hands of the son of Mother India. Charu was already in police custody. But the British government continued the same unspeakable torture and torture. Meanwhile, Charuchandra was adamant, unwavering. No information could be extracted from his mouth.

Then it was the turn of the trial, Charu was presented before the sessions judge in the court. Do you know what Charu Basu said there, he said - 'The sessions trial is meaningless. Let me be hanged tomorrow! Everything is predictable - Ashubabu will die by my bullet and I will hang myself. I killed him because he was an enemy of the country.' The trial ruled that Charuchandra Basu was sentenced to death. The death sentence was upheld. Despite Charu's many requests, he did not agree to appeal to the British court.

On March 19, 1909, Charuchandra Bose ascended the gallows at Alipore Central Jail. With great pride, he took the noose around his neck. At the age of just 20, Charuchandra Bose, despite being a rival, proved that Indians are not weak in any situation.

Charuchandra Bose

Charuchandra Bose was born in 1890 in the village of Shobhana in the then Khulna district. His father's name was Keshab Chandra Bose. He participated in the Swadeshi movement in the first decade and later became a member of the Anushilan Samiti.

Ashutosh Biswas was the lawyer for the British government in the Alipur and Muraripukur bomb cases and other cases. He actively helped collect evidence against various revolutionaries to ensure their punishment. He had to be killed at any cost. This task was entrusted to Charuchandra Bose.After this, Charuchandra Bose, carrying a pistol in his paralyzed right hand and wrapped in a shawl, headed towards the court premises. The day was 10th February 1909, when lawyer Ashutosh Biswas came out of the court, Charuchandra Bose's pistol went off. Ashutosh Biswas started screaming and running away, but more bullets came out of Charuchandra Bose's pistol. Ashutosh Biswas died on the spot. By then, a police team had surrounded him from all sides, and Charuchandra Bose was arrested.

The revolutionary youth was subjected to unspeakable torture, but the police could not extract anything from him. The court proceedings ended on February 22, 1909.

He was sentenced to death in the trial and on March 19, 1909, he sang the song of victory for life on the gallows at Alipore Central Jail.

CHAPTER FIVE

Sir Curzon Wyllie Assassination

The time was 1905, when the wave of rebellion and revolution swept across India. Then the sparks of this wave also swept across British soil. Many young Indians were then in British soil. Already, the expatriate revolutionary Shyamji Krishna Varma had established 'India House' abroad. This 'India House' was a boarding house for Indian students. From there, Shyamji Krishna Varma propagated the ideology of revolution. On the other hand, the British government started keeping a close watch on Shyamji Krishna Varma. The British government realized that through 'India House' he was indoctrinating young students in the revolutionary mantra. Then Shyamji Krishna Varma first went to Paris to avoid arrest and then to Switzerland.

Then the heroic revolutionary Vinayak Damodar Savarkar took over the leadership of 'India House'. The time was 1909, and his work became adventurous. There, members were secretly taught how to shoot pistols. At that time, the ADC of Lord Morley, the Secretary of State for India, was Sir William Curzon Wyllie. As per the government, he was given the responsibility of looking after the Indian students living in Britain. But far from looking after them, he was secretly given the responsibility of spying on them.

Already, Plague Commissioner Mr. Rand and Lieutenant Ayerst, then Ganesh Shankar Dravid and his brother Ramchandra Dravid's 'Chapekar friends' died on the gallows in the murder case. Damodar

Hari Chapekar, Balkrishna Hari Chapekar, Vasudev Hari Chapekar and Mahadev Vinayak Ranade. Then in Bengal, Prafulla Chaki and Khudiram Bose died on the gallows in the Kingsford murder case. Satyendranath Bose and Kanailal Dutt died on the gallows in the murder case of traitor Naren Gosai. Even then, British officer Sir Curzon Wyllie is keeping a close eye on Indian students.

Madanlal Dhingra was a student of 'India House'. He accepted the heroic revolutionary Damodar Savarkar as his political guru. As a student, Madanlal Dhingra was initiated into the revolutionary mantra by Savarkar. He took an oath - 'I will give a reply to this national insult to the people of India.' Now Sir Curzon Wyllie will be punished for spying on Indians. Madanlal Dhingra came forward for this task.

The day was 1st July 1909, a party was held at the Jahangir Mahal in London on the occasion of the annual festival by the 'National Association'. Curzon Wylie joined that party, and it was at that party that Madan Lal Dhingra's pistol roared. Curzon Wyllie lost his life in the gunshot that roared. Rajbhakt Parsi doctor Lal Kaka came forward to help the injuredCurzon Wyllie. He also lost his life in the gunshot of Madan Lal Dhingra.

It is surprising to think that an Indian can roar like a lion in a foreign land. He was immediately arrested. After his arrest, a piece of paper was found in Madan Lal Dhingra's pocket. It was written on that paper - 'As a feeble protest against the arbitrary imprisonment and death sentence of Indian youth, I have voluntarily tried to shed the blood of the British.' Madan Lal Dhingra was sentenced to death in the trial. He was hanged on 17 August 1909 in a London jail.

Madanlal Dhingra

Madanlal Dhingra was born in 1887 in Amritsar, Punjab. He received his early education in Lahore, he was not very interested in studies. He devoted himself more to bodybuilding. He passed his B.A. from Punjab University. He had to go to London for further studies. There, he joined as a member after establishing Shyamji Krishna Varma's 'India House'.

Madanlal Dhingra shot Sir Curzon Wyllie on 1 July 1909. Then he was arrested, and on 10 July he was produced in the magistrate's court. There, Madanlal Dhingra made a few comments, he said in a loud voice - 'Just as the Germans have no right to occupy Britain, Britain has no right to occupy India. This Britisher wants to defile my native land, India. Killing him is an order of justice for me. I am shocked by the hypocrisy, shameless lies, and sarcastic behavior of the British.

I believe that to keep a nation under the pressure of foreign bayonets is to force that nation to be constantly at war. But there is no room for open war. Because, our weapons have been taken away by law. So I attacked my enemy. I will not be given a pistol license, so in this case my secret pistol roared.'

He further said - 'India has only one lesson to learn at present - that is the lesson of death and there is only one method of teaching that lesson - the lesson of becoming fearless of death by dying myself. So I have died myself. May my sacrifice be victorious.'

Hearing this, many present there were filled with tears. At the end of it, he offered his last prayer to God - 'My only wish is that I may be born again and again in the womb of my pregnant mother and again and again embrace death in the pursuit of national liberation - until my Indian land is completely independent and established on the seat of glory in the world assembly.' Madanlal Dhingra was sentenced to death in the trial. On August 17, 1909, he was hanged in London, far away from his native land, India. This was the first revolutionary of India who had to die on the gallows far away from his native land.

CHAPTER SIX

A.M.T. Jackson Murder

Revolutionary organizations were formed one after another in Maharashtra. Three brothers of Chapekar died on the gallows in Maharashtra. When the time was in the Age of Fire, armed revolution was needed to snatch freedom. But how will the work of revolution be successful? As long as the oppression of the British government continues, some British officers are reaching their maximum limits. Meanwhile, their names have appeared in the diary of the revolution.

The revolutionary organization founded by the revolutionaries Ganesh Damodar Savarkar and Vinayak Damodar Savarkar was called 'Abhinav Bharat'. Many revolutionaries were associated with this organization, such as Anant Laxman Kanhere, Krishnagopal Karve and Vinayak Narayan Deshpande and many others. Meanwhile, the tyrannical British officer, the Collector of Nashik, A.M.T. Jackson, was increasing day by day. So this time the name of Jackson's murder came up in the revolutionary circle.

If Jackson cannot be removed from the world, the revolution will never succeed. According to the plan of the revolution hall, Anant Laxman Kanhere was given the responsibility of killing Jackson. Anant Laxman Kanhere was not sent alone, but was accompanied by Krishnagopal Karve and Vinayak Narayan Deshpande. Several other revolutionaries were present in this plan. It so happened that Jackson to at the Vijayanand Theatre in Nashik, where he would get the opportunity to kill him. Because Jackson was a great fan of the Marathi language, hc often went to see plays there.

The day was December 21, 1909, the last performance of the play 'Sharda' at the Vijayanand Theatre. Jackson was present in the theatre that day. Shortly after him, Ananta Laxman Kanhere, Krishnagopal Karve and Vinayak Narayan Deshpande arrived. As per their plan, Ananta Laxman would kill Jackson, while Krishnagopal and Vinayak Deshpande would hide in the darkness of the theatre. If by some mistake Ananta Laxman failed to kill Jackson, Krishnagopal and Vinayak Deshpande would move forward instead.

Then Anant fixed his aim and moved forward. He saw that Jackson was now in his grasp, this was his opportunity. Without delay, Anant opened fire on Jackson, while Krishnagopal and Vinayak Deshpande had their pistols ready. When Jackson tried to escape, Anant's pistol roared for the second time and immediately A.M.T. Jackson fell to the ground. He fired every bullet from the pistol at Jackson's body.

Anant was standing at his place, and then the police arrested him there. But Anant was supposed to commit suicide after work that day, unfortunately he did not get the chance. A massive crackdown began in Maharashtra at that time based on this incident. On December 22, 1909, Dattatreya Panduram Joshi and Ganesh B. Vaidya were arrested. On December 23, Vinayak Narayan Deshpande and Shankar Ramchandra Soman were arrested. The next day, on the 24th, Krishnagopal Karve was arrested. At the end of the month, on December 30, Vaman Narayan Joshi was arrested.

This time, a case of Jackson's murder was filed against all those revolutionaries in the Bombay High Court on March 20, 1910. The trial verdict sentenced Ananta Laxman Kanhere, Krishnagopal Karve and Vinayak Narayan Deshpande to death. Baman Narayan Joshi, Shankar Ramchandra Soman and Ganesh B. Vaidya were sentenced to life imprisonment. And the remaining one, Dattatreya Panduram Joshi, was sentenced to two years of rigorous imprisonment.

Then, exactly a month later, on April 19, 1910, three young men from Maharashtra, Ananta Laxman Kanhere, Krishnagopal Karve and Vinayak Narayan Deshpande, sang the song of life on the gallows. Even after this, the British government caused such a sad incident that the bodies of the three young men were not handed over to their relatives. The bodies of the three Sun children of the Agni Yuga were cremated in the middle of the jail.

These were the words of the three Agni Mahanayaks of the Jackson murder. They went to the gallows and proved that the brave sons of Mother India are never behind.

Ananta Laxman Kanhere

Ananta Laxman Kanhere was born on 7 January 1892 in Indore. They had two sisters and two brothers. He received his primary education in Indore and completed his secondary education in Aurangabad from his maternal uncle's house. His elder brother's name was Ganapati. His ancestor was a resident of Ratnagiri district. At that time, two phases were clearly visible in the struggle for freedom in India. The first phase was that the Congress was against armed struggle. Their struggle was non-violent.

The second phase of the struggle for freedom was armed struggle. The young people of that time thought that freedom could be achieved through arms. When in 1905 the British government created a distinction between Hindus and Muslims. Then it divided Bengal, as a result of this, the spark of intense revolution was ignited in the minds of the revolutionaries.

Ananta Laxman Kanhere went to Aurangabad with his uncle in 1903 for further education. His brother Ganapati also lived in Barshi. After staying with him for some time, he returned to Aurangabad in 1908 and lived as a tenant in the house of Gangaram Roopchand Shroff. Gangaram had a friend named Tonpe. He was a secret member of the revolutionary party in Nashik. A Ganu (Ganesh) doctor from Nashik used to go to Yella to meet his relative. Ganu met Gangaram in Yella. He went to Aurangabad with Gangaram to buy weapons for the Nashik Secret Society. Ananta Laxman Kanhere met this doctor in Aurangabad. Ananta Laxman

Kanhere once met a doctor. Later, Kanhere wrote a novel called 'Mitra Prem' about their friendship. Kanhere was attracted to the work of the revolutionary party. The Savarkar brothers founded the 'Abhinav Bharat' organization in Nashik. Krishnaji Gopal Karve Babarao formed such a secret group under the leadership of Savarkar. Another member of this organization was Vinayak Narayan Deshpande. Anant Kanhere was inspired by the Savarkar brothers.

In 1909, Jai Ganesh Savarkar was sentenced to life imprisonment for publishing various patriotic poems against the British government. This further enraged the revolutionaries. Soon after, Jackson was transferred to a higher post in Mumbai. It was easy to kill him in Nashik. The play 'Sharda' was staged for Jackson's farewell function at the Vijayanand Theatre in Nashik on 21 December 1909. There, Jackson was shot dead by Anant Kanhere. Krishnagopal Karve and Vinayak Narayan Deshpande were involved in this murder case.

On 20 March 1910, the court sentenced all three to death. Finally, on 19 April 1910, all three were hanged in the prison.

Krishnagopal Karve

Krishnagopal Karve was also known as 'Ana Karve'. Gopal Karve was a scholar of Hindu philosophy. He had a strong belief in the concept of reincarnation.

So he used to say about reincarnation, 'If I die soon, I will be reborn again and can start fighting the British again.' This great revolutionary was born in Nashik in 1887. He studied B.A. Honours, he was only 23 years old at that time.

After completing his B.A. Honours, he joined the L.L.B. course to study law at Bombay University. He was the brainchild of one of the secret organizations in Maharashtra. He joined the Abhinav Bharat Society in Nashik, a revolutionary organization founded by Ganesh Damodar Savarkar and Vinayak Damodar Savarkar, 'Abhinav Bharat'. He initiated Shankar, Ramchandra, Somen into revolution in the secret society. He also knew how to prepare bombs and taught those processes to Vaman Narayan Joshi and Ramchandra.

Krishnagopal Karve bought seven Browning pistols, one revolver and one country-made pistol from Gopal Rao Patankar. He was not only an active member of the 'Abhinav Bharat' Society in Nashik, Maharashtra, but he was also well known for the freedom movement in India. Accused of anti-British activities and sentiments, he formed a revolutionary party with other revolutionaries like Vinayak Narayan Deshpande, Baburao Savarkar and Vinayak Damodar Savarkar.

This time, the name of District Magistrate Jackson has been written in the Dairy of revolutionaries, Jackson was shot dead by Ananta Kanhere. Krishnagopal Karve and Vinayak Narayan Deshpande were involved in this murder case.

On March 20, 1910, the court sentenced all three to death. Finally, on April 19, 1910, all three were hanged in prison.

Gopal Karve was the only son of his parents. This supreme sacrifice of his brought an end to his dynasty.

Vinayak Narayan Deshpande

Vinayak Narayan Deshpande was a member of the secret revolutionary organization. He married at a young age. At one time he was the first assistant teacher of the Panchavati School in Nashik. As an additional occupation, he ran a loom. In the building where he was doing this additional work. There was an old dark room on the third floor, where Deshpande and other revolutionaries of the secret meeting also stayed occasionally.

Narayan Deshpande collected bomb-making materials (explosives) and spices, which were kept in a box. But unfortunately, nothing special is known about this great revolutionary. He was a member of the revolutionary organization 'Abhinav Bharat' founded by Ganesh Damodar Savarkar and Vinayak Damodar Savarkar. Meanwhile, the tyrannical British officer Collector A.M.T. Jackson of Nashik was increasing day by day. For that, Jackson was killed.

The High Court verdict was delivered on March 20, 1910. Vinayak Narayan Deshpande, Krishna Gopal Karve and Ananta Laxman Kanhere were sentenced to death.

Finally, on April 19, 1910, all three were hanged in the prison.

Baman Narayan Joshi

Baman Narayan Joshi was born in 1889 in the village of Akola, Shamsherpur, Ahmednagar district. He received his primary education in Shamsherpur and went to Nashik for further education. He was particularly inspired by the Savarkar brothers at that time. The British government imposed many restrictions on the Savarkar brothers and the Abhinav Bharat Sansthan. This led to growing resentment among Savarkar's followers. The Collector of Nashik at that time, Jackson, was responsible for this atrocity. As a result, it was decided to kill Jackson along with Baman Narayan Joshi, Vinayak Narayan Deshpande, Krishna Gopal Karve and Ananta Laxman Kanhere and other revolutionaries. The Nashik revolutionaries obtained Browning pistols ordered from Paris at that time for their plan. With the help of these pistols, Jackson was shot dead at the Vijayanand Theatre on 21 December 1909. At the end of the month, on December 30th, Vaman Narayan Joshi was arrested.

Baman Narayan Joshi was subjected to severe physical torture. In the Nashik Conspiracy Case - Baman Narayan Joshi was sentenced to life imprisonment under Sections 302/109, 121, 124 for the murder of District Magistrate Mr. Jackson in 1910. On 7 April 1911, he was sent to the Andaman Cellular Jail. In 1920, he was ordered to be brought back to an Indian jail. He was released from jail in 1922. Baman Narayan Joshi was also known as 'Dajikaka' in revolutionary circles.

Finally, on 14 January 1964, the revolutionary Baman Narayan Joshi breathed his last.

CHAPTER SEVEN

Shamsul Alam Murder

India might have gained independence long ago, But because some brokers were born in the heart of India, it took a long time to gain independence. One after another, the fiery Agnikishor revoluyionary of sang the song of victory for life on the gallows in order to gain freedom. These young men were framed by falsely accusing the revolutionaries. One of the people who fabricated these false cases was Shamsul Alam. In the Alipore bomb conspiracy case, the responsibility of fabricating false cases against the brave revolutionaries and passing off lies fell on Shamsul Alam. Shamsul was the right hand of the British government's attorney, Mr. Norton. The Deputy Superintendent has treated Shamsul like a king.

Shamsul Alam was used to frame cases against royal prisoners. He was skilled in passing off truth as lies and lies as truth, and in gathering royal witnesses. He took advantage of the weaknesses of young royal prisoners. He was excellent in various nefarious activities of the revolutionaries. Shamsul was a living document of the Alipore bomb conspiracy case. That is why Mr. Alam was blacklisted by the revolutionaries. There were two attempts to assassinate him before the Alipore bomb conspiracy case began, but Mr. Alam could not be found.

Shamsul Alam's life has expired, so he cannot be given the opportunity to do more. The revolutionaries composed a song about him - 'Oh Shamsul/You are the government's Shyam, our Shul/When will your cattle graze/You will see mustard flowers in your eyes'. Who will take responsibility for this murder? A 19-year-old young man, Biren Duttagupta (Birendranath Duttagupta), came forward. Jatindranath entrusted the responsibility of killing Shamsul Alam to his beloved disciple Birendra.

Now the day and time were set. The day was January 24, 1910, the brave young man Biren Duttgupta set out to kill Shamsul Alam. The clock struck 5.30 PM, Biren was waiting for Shamsul Alam outside the High Court. That day, Shamsul handed over the papers to the government lawyers and started walking. Shamsul was descending the stairs upstairs, accompanied by armed police.

Biren overcame all his fears and went towards Shamsul. Shamsul saw an unknown young man in the small gap. Within a moment, Biren's pistol roared with a loud noise, and within an instant, the British servant Mr. Alam fell down. Birendranath did this in front of many people, it was certain that after carrying out this murder in such a crowd, it was not possible to escape. Whoever did this, he had to be caught and getting caught was natural. That's right, Birendranath was caught.

Unspeakable torture were inflicted on Biren, who was imprisoned in jail, but Biren did not open his mouth for anything. Despite many attempts, no information could be extracted from Biren's mouth. During the trial, Biren did not take the help of any lawyer or barrister. The trial ordered his execution, and finally, on February 21, 1910, Birendranath Duttagupta, the fiery son of Bengal, sang the song of life on the gallows.

Birendranath Duttagupta

Biren was born on 20 June 1889 in Baligaon village of Bikrampur, Dhaka. His father's name was Umacharan and his mother's name was Basanta Kumari Devi. Biren was the second child of his parents, his father died at a very young age. In 1908, Biren was admitted to Jalpaiguri District School as a ninth-grade student. Then he moved to Kolkata. Biren, inspired by the ideals of the deceased Kanailal Dutta, got involved in revolutionary activities. He chose

Jatindranath Mukherjee alias Bagha Jatin as his revolutionary path guru.

On January 24, 1910, he was arrested while trying to kill Shamsul Alam. Despite much torture by the police, Biren did not reveal any secret information. Justice Lawrence Jenkins appointed Barrister Nishith Sen as the defense counsel. But Biren did not say a single word to Nishith Sen, fearing that the secret information of the revolutionaries would be leaked. In the end, Biren was sentenced to death in the trial. In the meantime, the British government hatched a heinous conspiracy to extract secret information from Biren.

When Biren was not opening his mouth, the British government planned a heinous plot. Biren, who was imprisoned, was handed over a fake newspaper of revolutionary party, since it never belonged to the revolutionary party. In that paper, Bagha Jatin's (Jatindranath Mukherjee) statement was written - Birendranath Duttagupta killed Shamsul Alam, and he is responsible for this. The dying Biren finally broke down and committed revolutionary betrayal like Jatin Mukherjee. Biren could not guess the details of this police plot.

Viren was completely devastated, and finally Jatin da did this. To clear this taint, Biren confessed that he had killed Shamsul as ordered by Jatindranath. Then Bagha Jatin was arrested, and since witness Biren had been hanged earlier, the British government could not provide any evidence. Jatin was forced to be released as per the court order. Finally, on February 21, 1910, Birendranath Duttagupta was hanged in the present-day Alipore Presidency Jail.

CHAPTER EIGHT

Tirunelveli District Collector Ashe Murder

A wave of rebellion descended on Madras, The revolutionaries there witnessed the torture of Bipin Chandra Pal and moved forward on the path of revolution. In 1907, Bipin Chandra Pal was sentenced to six months in prison for contempt of court by District Magistrate Kingsford. This torture on Bipin Chandra Pal created a stir in the revolutionary circles all over India. Bipin Chandra became the Lion of Swaraj in the heart of Madras. Chidambaram Pillai and Subrahmanya Shivam were initiated into the revolutionary mantra in the entire land of Madras, from the revolutionary Taraknath Das. They used to give speeches in front of the public at various places and talk about the torture of Bipin Chandra Pal. They said one thing against the British - 'Full Swaraj is our only desire, there will not be even a shadow of the British there.'

The British could not tolerate these activities of the revolutionaries. Therefore, the revolutionaries Chidambaram Pillai and Subrahmanyasivam were arrested. As a result, movements were seen in various places, riots started. Widespread arrests began across the country, secret manifestos and newspapers were being distributed. As a result of Chidambaram Pillai's arrest, a newspaper called 'Raj' was published in Bezwada. The British government banned the newspaper. The revolutionaries did not back down either. In 1908, Tinnevelly District Collector Ashe did not put an end to the atrocities in his attempt to suppress the rebellion of the revolutionaries. The revolutionaries became even more angry with Ash's atrocities. "We will avenge it," words left a black mark on the murder of Ashe in the revolutionaries' diary.

V.V.S., a revolutionary member of the 'India House' founded by Shyamji Krishna Varma in London in 1910, returned to India in 1911 and took refuge in Pondicherry. From there, he taught revolutionary youth how to shoot pistols. On the other hand, Nilkanth Iyer 'Brahmachari' and Shankar Krishna Iyer started spreading the message of revolution in various parts of southern India. Vanchi Iyer of Travancore joined their group. Vanchi Iyer secretly met the revolutionary V.V.S. and also planned. Ashe, the District Collector of Tirunelveli, had to be killed at any cost.

An anonymous letter was also sent to Mr. Ashe on behalf of the 'Bharat Mata Association', which read - 'Listen to the warning of the Bharat Mata Association. Do not meddle in any public affairs, if you disobey our prohibition message, I will cut off your head in an instant.' But Ashe did not pay any attention to this letter, he did not think it was a rebellious order.

On June 17, 1911, the Ashe couple left Tirunelveli by train. They changed trains at Manyanchi Junction and took a train to Kodaikanal. Vanchi Iyer and Shankar Krishna Iyer followed them. Ashe was sitting in the train carriage, this was the opportunity to kill Ashe. Suddenly of the moment, Vanchi Iyer's pistol roared, and Ash's lifeless body immediately fell into the train carriage. Then Wanchi Iyer and Shankar Krishna Iyer disappeared in of the moment. But to avoid arrest, Wanchi Iyer fired his pistol With at Gribadesh.

Then the police started a massive raid all around. Dharmaraj Iyer, Neelkanth Iyer 'Brahmachari' and Venkateswar Iyer and many other revolutionaries were caught. In the trial, each one was sentenced to various degrees.

Vanchi Iyer

Vanchi Iyer was born in 1886. His real name was Sankaran, but he was known as Vanchi. His father's name was Raghunath Iyer and his mother's name was Rukmani Devi. Vanchi Iyer was a government employee in the Forest Department. When V. V. S. came to Pondicherry, India and took refuge, Vanchi Iyer took a three-month leave to visit him. Before that, he was initiated into the revolutionary mantra by Neelkanth Iyer 'Brahmachari', and Shankarakrishna Iyer.

The revolutionary Vanchi Iyer and V. V. S. and other revolutionaries planned to assassinate District Collector Ashe. On 17th June 1911, Vanchi Iyer shot and killed District Collector Ashe.

He then left a paper on Ash's body, which was written in Tamil.

The author Jayantkumar Ghosh's book The Legend of Agniyug states, "Every Indian has thus striven to drive out the British and establish India's independence and Sanatan Dharma. Once upon a time, Sri Ramachandra, Sri Krishna, Shivaji, Guru Gobind Singh and Arjuna ruled this vast land of India. And today, the British are coronating a beef-eating Mlechha named George V in this vast land of India. Three thousand Madrasis have taken an oath that the moment George V sets foot on this vast land, they will kill George V. The murder of Ashe is just a premonition of that."

That day, after killing Ashe, Vanchi Iyer committed suicide by shooting himself.

Venkateshwar Iyer and Dharmaraj Iyer

When the investigation into the Ashe murder began, many young men were arrested. Among them were Venkateshwar Iyer and Dharmaraj Iyer, against Their the Tirunelveli Conspiracy Case' was started. During the trial, Venkateshwar Iyer and Dharmaraj Iyer committed suicide in custody in October 1911. They probably knew in advance what their sentence would be, so they committed suicide before hearing the verdict. The rest were sentenced to various terms by the Special Tribunal of the Madras High Court.

Neelkanth Iyer 'Brahmachari'

Neelkanth Iyer was one of the leaders of the Madras Revolutionary Party. He spread the message of revolution in the Madras region and inspired the youth with the revolutionary mantra. He initiated Vanchi Iyer of Travancore into the revolutionary fire mantra. When Vanchi Iyer shot and killed District Collector Ashe on June 17, 1911, the British started arresting in various parts based on this incident.

Revolutionary Neelkanth Iyer was arrested, the historic case 'Tirunelveli Conspiracy Case' began. Neelkanth Iyer was accused as the main accused in this case. He was sentenced to seven years of rigorous imprisonment in the trial.

CHAPTER NINE

Nirad Halder and Suresh Mukherjee Murders

On 12 February 1915, revolutionaries looted 18,000 taka from the British Bird Company in Garden Reach, Kolkata to advance the cause of the revolution. The main participant in this act was Narendranath Bhattacharya alias Manabendranath Roy, who did this act with Chittapriya Roychowdhury, a colleague of Purna Chandra Das' revolutionary party in Madaripur, and other revolutionaries. Exactly ten days later, revolutionaries looted 22,000 taka from the house of Vrindavan Saha in Beleghata. Chittapriya Roychowdhury, Manoranjan, Niren and Fani Chakraborty participated in this act. The Kolkata police became active in the incident of two robberies in a row.

On February 24, 1915, the revolutionaries carried out many raids and looted a lot of money to use for the revolution, and the money was distributed in the Pathuriaghata area of Kolkata. There was a house there that had been empty for a long time, where the revolutionaries used to import weapons. From there, weapons were sent to various centers of the revolutionaries. There was a paanwala's shop at the intersection, the paanwala guessed that something illegal was going on here. So he informed the intelligence officer Nirad Halder through a secret source. But that day, there were a few more revolutionaries there.

Intelligence officer Nirad Halder, upon receiving the news, wanted to know what was happening in that house, so he went out to investigate. He entered the house as if Nirad Halder was entering the house of a familiar person. As soon as he entered the house, he saw Bagha Jatin himself. Chittapriya thinks? Bagha Jatin himself will eventually be caught by an ordinary detective. So, without wasting any more time, Chittapriya took out the loaded pistol from his pocket and started shooting.

His name and address were found in the pocket of the bullet-scarred Nirad Haldar. As per the party's instructions, Nirad Haldar used to send some money to his wife at his house every month. But Nirad Haldar did not die immediately after being shot by Chittapriya. He was admitted to the hospital and Nirad Haldar only mentioned Bagha Jatin's name in his statement. Since then, they have faced various obstacles.

The notorious Tagart Sahib was the Police Commissioner of Kolkata at that time. Strict surveillance was kept in Kolkata city, this robbery was done on the orders of Jatindranath Mukherjee (Bagha Jatin). To fulfill the dream of all-out revolution, a lot of money was needed, so the revolutionaries chose this path. At one time, the revolutionary Narendranath Bhattacharjee was arrested by the police. As soon as he saw Narendranath, Detective Inspector Suresh Mukherjee arrested him. The plan that Bagha Jatin had made about Narendranath, turned out to be a failure. Bagha Jatin was supposed to send Narendranath abroad to import weapons.

This time, Narendranath must be freed from the police by any means. It was reported that Narendranath would be taken from Lalabazar to some other place. To take advantage of this opportunity, the young men, on Jatin's orders, set off towards Lalbazar with pistols in their hands. As per the orders, as soon as they saw Narendranath, they stopped the police car and snatched their comrade. But their attempt to wait in front of Lalbazar that day failed. According to secret sources, Narendranath was secretly sent to Alipore jail last night.

Jatin was furious, "If Narendranath cannot be freed, all my plans will be in vain. I want to see Suresh Mukherjee's death and his blood today, otherwise I will not even take a glass of water." Seeing

Bagha Jatin's promise, Chittapriya and the other four revolutionary companions left. Meanwhile, Barolart is coming to Calcutta University, Suresh Mukherjee is busy with him. The police are keeping a sharp eye on all sides. Chittapriya and his four companions moved forward past the police surveillance. Already after the death of Nirad Haldar, Chittapriya's picture is being distributed here and there in the intelligence office, there is an order to arrest him as soon as he is seen.

Once, as soon as Suresh Mukherjee saw Chittapriya, he went forward to arrest him. Suresh asked Chittapriya, 'Are you not Chittapriya?' Chittapriya replied, 'Yes, I am the Chittapriya.' Far from arresting him, Suresh Mukherjee fell to the ground as soon as the revolutionary's pistol roared. After that, he fulfilled the promise of Bagha Jatin by applying Suresh Mukherjee's blood to the tip of the pistol. After that, the revolutionaries disappeared. After that, Jatin succeeded in rescuing Narendranath after making various plans.

Chittapriya Roychowdhury

Chittapriya Roychowdhury was born on 6 December 1894 in a landlord family in Khalia village of Madaripur. His father's name was Panchanan Roychowdhury and his mother's name was Sukhada Sundari Devi. His father Panchanan Roychowdhury was an honorary magistrate in Madaripur city.

Chittapriya Roychowdhury first studied at Thalia High School. Later, he was admitted to Madaripur High School. While at Madaripur High School, he became a member of the Madaripur Samiti (Revolutionary Party) in 1910. Chittapriya Roychowdhury, as a colleague of the great revolutionary Purna Chandra Das, became a member of the secret revolutionary organization run by Purna Chandra. In December 1913, Chittapriya Roychowdhury was identified as an accused in the first Faridpur Conspiracy Case. He was arrested and imprisoned for five months before being released from jail.

After being released from jail, Chittapriya Roychowdhury killed Suresh Mukherjee, a police inspector on duty, on the convocation day of Calcutta University on 28 February 1915, with the help of some colleagues. As a colleague of revolutionary Jatin Mukherjee (Bagha Jatin), Chittapriya Roychowdhury tried to import weapons from Germany, Japan, America and the Dutch Indies. On 7 September 1915, Bagha Jatin (Jatin Mukherjee) returned to his temporary hideout in Mahaldiha late at night. Chittapriya Roychowdhury, Jyotish Chandra Pal, Manoranjan Sengupta and Nirendranath Dasgupta were with him.

Chittapriya Roychowdhury, Bagha Jatin and the rest of their companions spent the whole day of September 8 in their deep forest. Walking all night, they reached the outskirts of the Buribalam river in Balasore in the early morning of September 9. They swam across the river and took shelter in a dry pond that was quite suitable for war. On the opposite side, Charles Tegart, Commander Rutherford, District Magistrate Kilvee appeared with numerous armed police and military forces. Five men led by Bagha Jatin, with Mauzer pistols in their hands.

This was the last battle in the life of Chittapriya Roychowdhury. On one side, only 5 people and on the other, numerous soldiers. Now the historic battle of Buribalam began, firing in response to firing. The 5 of them started firing together. So that the enemy side would not know how many of them there were. Several British soldiers were killed. Until the end, the revolutionaries were firing at the end. The battle went on for quite some time, at that moment, the police bullets hit Chittapriya Roychowdhury. Chittapriya fell to the ground, the battle was still going on. In a voice of pain, he said - 'Barada, I am leaving.'

On the road to death traveler, chittapriya was panting for a drop of water. Meanwhile, Bagha Jatin was also shot. But he is supposed to fight to the end, To give water to Chittapriya, he waved his blood-stained white shirt, signaling a ceasefire and surrendering. The British Sahib approached, and Bagha Jatin said in a deep voice - "I am stopping the fight just to give him a drop of water." Shortly after, the young Kishore Chittapriya breathed his last. The day was September 9, 1915. Chittapriya died like a hero in the Chaskhande of Buribalam.

CHAPTER TEN

Mr. Day was killed in an attempt to kill Tegart

Tegart Saheb was a police commissioner of the intelligence department of Kolkata at that time. He was a very intelligent and skilled British royal. He had a sharp eye on the revolutionaries, Tegart was a notorious police officer to the revolutionaries. His torture on the revolutionaries is increasing day by day. Tegart Saheb has become a monster. In every case of revolutionaries, it is seen that they plan to kill the enemy in groups. But here the opposite was seen. A young man named Gopinath Saha decided alone that he would kill Tegart Saheb alone.

The day was January 12, 1924, and Deshbandhu Chittaranjan Das was busy with many papers at home. Deshbandhu Chittaranjan Das was a renowned barrister at that time. Meanwhile, Gopinath Saha, with a pistol tied to his waist, set off for Deshbandhu Chittaranjan Das' house. He had gone to Deshbandhu's house to seek his blessings. Gopinath considered him his Gurudev. Since Gopinath was going to kill Tegart Saheb, how could he go out without the Gurudev's footsteps and blessings? Meanwhile, Deshbandhu was very busy with papers. Gopinath Saha, however, did not tell Gurudev anything about the Tegart murder. So Deshbandhu did not even have a clue what Gopi was going to do.

Gopi's conversation with Deshbandhu has irritated Deshbandhu. Deshbandhu was too busy to answer, so Gopi said, "Then I'm going, bless me." Deshbandhu didn't listen to this, so Gopi said once more

- "I'm leaving." Gopinath was a very close person to Deshbandhu, so he affectionately called Gopinath his Fire Brand son. Now Deshbandhu looked up from the paper and said, "Where are you going?" Gopinath smiled and replied, "That's what I said." Gopinath Deshbandhu had no recollection of what he had said. The boy was bothering him a lot during work, so he said - 'Go! Go wherever you want.' After saying this, Gopinath left with the dust of Deshbandhu's footsteps, his joy knew no bounds. It was his only misfortune to receive an order from Gurudev himself.

Gopinath went to the same route that Tegart used to travel and waited at the junction of Chowringhee Park Street. After waiting for a long time, Tegart Sahib was found. Within a moment, Gopinath Saha's pistol roared, and the shot man fell to his death. Gopinath was overjoyed to see that the plan to kill Tegart had succeeded. Gopinath was immediately arrested, but Tegart Sahib did not die from Gopi's pistol shot. Mr. Day Sahib died by mistake. Gopinath broke down after knowing this truth, Mr. Tegart survived.

The trial began soon after, and Gopinath Saha was sentenced to death. Gopi said only one thing that day - "I am saddened by the death of Dey Saheb. I regret that Tegart survived. I hope that someone is not behind to complete my incomplete work." On March 1, 1924, Gopinath Saha sacrificed his life on the gallows.

Gopinath Saha

Gopinath Saha was born on 7 December 1906 in Serampore, Hooghly. His father's name was Vijay Krishna Saha. Gopinath was forced to leave school during the Non-Cooperation Movement and gradually worked with various leaders of revolutionary organizations such as Hooghly Vidyamandir, Calcutta Saraswati Library and Saraswati Press, Daulatpur Satyashram, Barisal Shankara Math, Uttarpara Vidyapeeth etc. At that time, the tyrannical Calcutta Police Commissioner Charles Tegart had become a monster to the revolutionaries. One day, Gopinath made preparations to remove Charles Tegart from the world. The year was 1924 and it was at this time that Gopinath fully joined the revolutionary movement. On January 12, 1924, at the junction of Chowringhee and Park Street, Ernest Day was shot dead, mistaking him for Mr. Tegart. The trial ordered Gopinath to be hanged, and finally Gopinath was hanged on March 1, 1924. Deshbandhu was deeply hurt by Gopinath's hanging.

Gopinath Saha consoled his mother and said before his execution, "That you are my mother. This is your glory. There is nothing to bewail. Let every mother give birth to a courageous son of your type and this illumine the face of mother India."

Bhupen Chatterjee Murder in Alipore Jail

The day was 10th November 1925, the police raided the secret bases of the revolutionaries in Dakshineswar. Almost everyone there, including the revolutionary leader Harinarayan Chanda, was arrested by the police. The house where they were arrested was their bomb-making factory. The police searched the house and recovered all the materials for making bombs. During the search, the police found another revolutionary site in Shobhabazar. When the secret hideout of the revolutionaries in Dakshineswar was searched, revolutionary Chaitanyadev Chatterjee was present in the house next door. Since he was in the house next door, he was not caught, he knew that the That police This time would raid the revolutionary center in Shobhabazar. Chaitanyadev rushed to the Shobhabazar Revolutionary Asthana to report the news. But they were not informed again.

Revolutionary greats Masterda Surya Sen, Pramodranjan Chowdhury and Ananta Chakraborty were present there. The revolutionaries also knew that there was no escape, Masterda Suryasen left with dust in the eyes of the police. Masterda came out with a tea kettle in his hand, dressed as a tea vendor, and no one could even know. And finally Pramodranjan Chowdhury and Ananta Chakraborty were caught by the police. After searching there, the police found two caliber cartridges, a pistol and various papers related to the revolution.

The accused in the Dakshineswar bomb case are Harinarayan Chanda, Anantahari Mitra, Rajen Lahiri, Pramodranjan Chowdhury and Ananta Chakraborty. The trial sentenced three of them to ten years rigorous imprisonment - Harinarayan Chanda, Anantahari Mitra and Rajen Lahiri. The remaining two - Pramodranjan Chowdhury and Ananta Chakraborty - were sentenced to five years rigorous imprisonment. The rest were sentenced to three years each. They were then sent to Alipore Jail.

In Alipore Jail, Bhupen Chatterjee was seen entering the cells of the revolutionaries and communicating with them. Bhupen Chatterjee's aim was to break the morale of those who were a little raw and to extract secret information from their mouths. He tried to blend in with the revolutionaries, and he was a skilled person in this. Bhupen Chatterjee was the Special SP of 'RB'. The British government, was happy to break the morale of the revolutionaries and extract secret information, and awarded him the title of 'Rai Bahadur'. But how long will this trickery continue against the revolutionaries, now the name of Bhupen Chatterjee, i.e. the murder of Bhupen Chatterjee, has appeared in the register of imprisoned revolutionaries.

The revolutionaries planned to kill Bhupen Chatterjee in the jail, and they did not delay in doing so. The day was May 28, 1926, in the afternoon, Bhupen Chatterjee was going out to communicate with the revolutionaries as usual. Meanwhile, the revolutionaries were also ready. Knowing the time, Bhupen was caught, and just then Pramodranjan Chowdhury hit Bhupen hard with an iron rod. Bhupen Chatterjee immediately felt the pangs of death. There was an uproar all around, the jail bell rang. Bhupen Chatterjee was killed in the jail.

The trial began soon after, but no one agreed to testify against the revolutionaries. Finally, the British government tricked some foreign prisoners and Finningi prisoners into providing fabricated witnesses. The foreign and Finningi prisoners testified to the police's fabrications. It did not take long for the verdict to be announced. Pramodranjan Chowdhury and Anantahari Mitra were sentenced to death. Rakhal Dey, Dhruvesh Chatterjee and Ananta Chakraborty were sentenced to life imprisonment.

On September 28, 1926, the voices of all the prisoners in Alipore Central Jail echoed 'Vande Mataram'. Two young men, Pramodranjan Chowdhury and Anantahari Mitra, climbed the gallows.

Anantahari Mitra

Anantahari Mitra was born in 1906 in Nadia, undivided Bengal. His father's name was Rampal Mitra. The fire of independence was kindled in Anantahari Mitra's heart from his childhood. At the age of just 16, he joined the Non-Cooperation Movement in 1921 and was arrested. From then on, Ananta changed even more, after being released from jail, he joined the armed revolutionary group. Freedom will not come by word of mouth, freedom has to be snatched away.

From Krishnanagar, he moved to Kolkata, where he joined the Red Bengal Party. Ananta became active in the revolutionary cause and participated in various revolutionary activities. He became a favorite of the revolutionaries in a short time. To make the revolution successful, weapons were needed, so Anantahari Mitra and several revolutionaries committed a robbery in Krishnanagar. They said that they would not loot the houses of the poor, but if they wanted to loot, they would loot the British.

The police suspected Anantahari of committing a robbery in Krishnanagar, and Anantahari fled Krishnanagar and took refuge in Dakshineswar's house. On November 10, 1925, the police raided the house and arrested Anantahari Mitra and many others. The 'Dakshineswar Bomb Case' began. He was sentenced to ten years in prison in the trial. He was then taken to Alipore Central Jail.

In jail, on May 28, 1926, he and Pramodranjan Chowdhury killed Bhupen Chatterjee. After this murder, he was sentenced to death in a trial. At the age of just 20, Anantahari Mitra was hanged with on September 28, 1926.

Pramodranjan Chowdhury

Pramodranjan Chowdhury was born in 1904 in the village of Kelishahar in Chittagong. His father's name was Shri Ishan Chandra Chowdhury. In 1920, he was able to contact the revolutionaries while studying in school. He was a student of Chittagong Municipal School and was a close associate of Masterda Surya Sen, the great leader of the Chittagong Youth Uprising.

Pramodranjan Chowdhury joined the revolutionary party Anushilan Samiti while in school. He was one of the best students in the school. Ananta Singha was his classmate in the Chittagong Youth Uprising. It was Pramodranjan Chowdhury who first introduced Ananta Singha to Masterda Surya Sen. In 1921, Pramodranjan participated in the Non-Cooperation Movement.

On 10th November 1925, he was arrested in the Dakshineswar bomb case and sentenced to 5 years rigorous imprisonment. He was then sent to Alipore jail. On 28th May 1926, Anantahari Mitra and Pramod Chowdhury, who were convicted in the Dakshineswar bomb case, killed Bhupen Chatterjee with an iron rod in Alipore jail. Five revolutionaries were present at the incident.

Pramodranjan Chowdhury was sentenced to death for the murder of Bhupen Chatterjee, and was hanged on 28th September 1927.

Dhruvesh Chatterjee

Dhruvesh Chatterjee was born in Kolkata in 1904. His father's name was Pranavesh Chatterjee. Dhruvesh Chatterjee lost his father and mother in his childhood, after which he went to his maternal uncle's house in Uttarpara, Hooghly. His grandfather was the famous author of the best Bengali calendar, his name was Madhav Chandra Chatterjee.

Dhruvesh Chatterjee gradually dedicated himself to the Swadeshi movement. After that, he joined the Uttarpara Swadeshi

Yuva Samiti of the great revolutionary Amarendranath Chatterjee. While participating in various movements and with revolutionaries, he came in contact with the revolutionaries of Chittagong.

After some time, Dhruvesh Chatterjee started going to Dakshineswar Astana. Another notable incident is that Dhruvesh Chatterjee had saved some money for his sister's marriage. He donated the saved money to make bombs in Dakshineswar.

On 10th November 1925, the police raided the revolutionary headquarters in Shobhabazar. As a result, several revolutionaries and Dhruvesh Chatterjee were arrested along with illegal documents. On trial, he and nine revolutionaries were sentenced to seven years rigorous imprisonment. They were then kept in Alipore Jail.

In Alipore Jail, he was involved in the murder of Detective Inspector Bhupen Chatterjee, in which Anantahari Mitra and Pramodranjan Chowdhury were sentenced to death. Dhruvesh Chatterjee, Rakhal Dey and Ananta Chakraborty were sentenced to life imprisonment. After going on a hunger strike in Alipore Jail for a few days, he was sent to Mandalay Jail. Then in 1933, he was sent to Cellular Jail.

Dhruvesh Chatterjee was released from prison in 1937. But his health deteriorated due to the long imprisonment and he died on April 15, 1938.

Ananta kumar Chakraborty (Bholada)

Revolutionary Ananta kumar Chakraborty was the fourth person to assassinate Bhupen Chatterjee. He was born on 15 April 1901 in the village of Rakudia in Barisal district. He was the son of a middle-class family. His father's name was Chandramani Chakraborty. Ananta kumar, as a school student at the age of 14, joined the Shankar Math and Jugantar Dal of revolutionary Satish Chandra Mukherjee of Barisal.

Ananta kumar Chakraborty first worked at Daulatpur Satyashram, then he joined revolutionary activities in Kolkata for some time. Then he was introduced to the Dakshineswar Revolutionary Party. Together with the Jugantar Group, they worked to collect arms and ammunition from their hideouts in Dakshineswar and Shobhabazar. In connection with all this, Anantkumar and Pramod Chowdhury were arrested from Shobhabazar in the early hours of 10th November 1925 along with bomb-making chemicals and some documents.

He was sentenced to 5 years rigorous imprisonment in a special tribunal on 15 January 1926. He was imprisoned in Alipore Central Jail along with other revolutionaries in the Dakshineswar bomb case. Ananta kumar participated in the murder of Intelligence Officer Bhupendranath Chatterjee inside the jail. When Superintendent Bhupen Chatterjee was killed, Anantkumar Chakraborty was sentenced to life imprisonment in the murder case.

He was sent to Burma from Alipore Jail, and was imprisoned in various jails in Burma for 6 years. Then in 1933 he was sent to Cellular Jail. Ananta kumar was released from jail in 1938. Finally, on 5 June 1979, revolutionary Ananta kumar Chakraborty breathed his last.

CHAPTER TWELVE

Saunders Murder

The 'Simon Commission' entered India in 1928. As a result, public protests started in many places. The countrymen were not at all willing to accept the 'Simon Commission'. This effect was felt in Lahore, on October 30, 1928, Bhagat Singh, Rajguru and other revolutionaries joined the protest as per Lala Lajpat Rai's words. The only slogan that resounded in the voices of all freedom-loving countrymen was 'Simon Go Bag', Simon, you go back. Sometimes the slogan of the revolutionaries was 'Inclab Zindabad.'

Apart from Bhagat Singh, all the revolutionaries who were in this procession would protest as Lala Lajpat Rai had said, no fighting. In the meantime, the British government had issued a ban on all processions. The government would not allow any public gathering in public places. Meanwhile, the people would not obey the black laws they had given. That day, the sky and air chanted 'Simon Go Bag'. Seeing the fear of the people, the police were forced to enter the field, but the British police could not stop them.

This time during the procession, Lahore Police Superintendent Mr. Scott ordered a baton charge on the crowd. As soon as Scott gave the order, the armed police force jumped on the crowd. The baton was used on the common people indiscriminately, at one point this blow fell on the 'Punjab Keshari' Lala Lajpat Rai. The police team continued to hit Lalaji's head one after another. Finally, Lala Lajpat Rai fell down with a bloody body, while undergoing treatment, 'Punjab Keshari' Lala Lajpat Rai breathed his last on November 17, 1928.

This time the revolutionaries became even more furious at the death of the great revolutionary leader Lala Lajpat Rai. The revolutionaries saw with their own eyes that the Superintendent of Police Mr. Scott himself attacked Lala Lajpat Rai with a stick. This time Bhagat Singh and his other revolutionary companions sat down for a discussion. They had only one thing in mind, that the death of Lala Lajpat Rai must be avenged at any cost. "I want blood for blood, I will not spare those who killed Lalaji." Revolutionaries like Bhagat Singh, Shukdev, Rajguru and Chandrashekhar Azad came forward.

The revolutionary members of the 'Hindustan Republican Association Party' planned to kill Scott, to attack him just when he was leaving the office. The revolutionaries were keeping a close watch on Scott, what he had done and where he was going. Then the day approached. On December 14, 1928, Sukhdev went and stood in front of Scott's office. Bhagat Singh and his companions were a little distance away. After waiting for some time, a British officer was seen coming out of the office. Then that officer came out on a motorcycle. Then the revolutionaries went and stood in front of him, after which the revolutionaries' pistols roared. But Mr. Scott did not come that day, Assistant of Police Saunders came.

Sanders fell down there under the bullets of the revolutionaries, hearing the sound of the gunshots, a sergeant and his bodyguard Chandan Singh came running. Chandrashekhar Azad now took up arms and fired at Chandan Singh, Chandan Singh fell face down in his bullets. Scott was sitting in the office for work that day. After this incident, the revolutionaries disappeared. Bhagat Singh, Rajguru and a few other revolutionaries moved to Kolkata with the help of Durga Bhabir (Durgavati Devi). The rest scattered to various places.

After Bhagat Singh came to Kolkata with the help of Durga Bhabhi, he met several revolutionaries of Bengal and returned to Lahore with several weapons. This time, a bigger blow will have to be dealt to the British power, so he has to become stronger. Independence will not come easily, the right price will have to be paid for it. Several urgent bills will be discussed in the Delhi Assembly. The revolutionaries protested against these bills. They said that bombs will explode, but no one will die.

On June 6, 1929, Mr. Simon and Speaker Vallabhbhai Patel were sitting in the audience for the discussion of the Emergency Bill in the Parliament House in Delhi. Two strong young men, Bhagat Singh and Batukeshwar Dutt, arrived at the Parliament House. At one point, seeing an empty space, the two strong young men threw bombs, as promised, without any casualties. After that, they scattered bunches of red manifestos throughout the Assembly Hall. The Parliament House was filled with smoke. The revolutionaries aimed to protest on behalf of India against the Public Safety Bill.

Bhagat Singh and Batukeshwar Dutt started shouting slogans like "Inclab Zindabad" while distributing the manifesto. The two revolutionaries were arrested voluntarily, after this incident the whole country was shocked. A massive crackdown started, revolutionaries like Rajguru, Shukdev and Jatin Das were arrested. About 40 revolutionaries were arrested. The trial started, the verdict of the trial of the 'Lahore Conspiracy Case' and the Sanders murder case was pronounced on 27th October 1929. The trial ordered the death penalty for Bhagat Singh, Rajguru and Shukdev. The rest were sentenced in various stages.

On March 23, 1931, Bhagat Singh, Sukhdev Thapar and Shivram Rajguru were hanged in Lahore Central Jail. The countrymen could not even know about this incident, the three were hanged. Because the court had fixed the date of execution as March 24, the British government, fearing the people, hanged the three youths the previous day.

Bhagat Singh

Bhagat Singh was born on 28 September 1907 in the village of Bhanga in Lalpur district of undivided Punjab. His father's name was Sardar Kishan Singh. In 1919, thousands of people were killed at Jallianwala Bagh under the leadership of the infamous British officer O'Dwyer. Bhagat Singh suffered a lot after this incident.

While at Lahore National College, he came into contact with revolutionary leaders Bhai Parmanand and Sachindranath Sanyal. Bhagat Singh accepted them as his political gurus. Then he joined the armed revolutionary group. When the Simon Commission came to Lahore on 30th October 1928, the procession movement started. During the movement, Lala Lajpat Rai was hit by a heavy stick, and Lala Lajpat lost consciousness due to the impact. Lala Lajpat Rai died after 17 days during treatment, i.e. on 17th November. To avenge the murder of Lalaji, revolutionaries like Bhagat Singh, Rajguru, Chandrashekhar Azad killed Saunders instead of Scott.

Then Bhagat Singh and Batukeshwar Dutt threw bombs at the Parliament House in Delhi. Bhagat Singh was arrested and sentenced to death in the trial for the murder of Sanders and the 'Lahore Conspiracy Case'. Bhagat Singh, Sukhdev and Rajguru were hanged in Lahore Jail on 23 March 1931.

Singing the life on the gallows, the revolutionary Bhagat Singh is forever remembered in the hearts of the people of India with this.

Shivaram Rajguru

Shivaram Rajguru was born on 24 August 1908 in the village of Ghera in Pune district of Maharashtra. His father's name was Hari Narayan Rajguru. Shivaram Rajguru left home in 1924 at the age of 16 without informing anyone to travel to India. After some time, he also taught in a primary school. Then at the age of 18, he joined the revolutionary party. Then he came in contact with the revolutionary hero Bhagat Singh.

In 1927, the British government was about to issue a law called the Simon Commission. There was a strong protest against this commission because it did not include any Indian members. Wherever this commission went, the slogans were raised - 'Go Bag Simon.'

October 30, 1928. The whole of Punjab was in turmoil that day, Punjab Keshari Lala Lajpat Rai came out to protest the commission.

He was injured by the brutal baton charge of the police force and breathed his last 17 days later. A police officer named Mr. Scott was the main responsible for this murder. Rajguru, Bhagat Singh and other revolutionaries planned to kill Scott. While trying to kill Scott, the revolutionaries accidentally killed DSP Saunders. After this, Rajguru jumped into revolutionary work with new enthusiasm. He formed a revolutionary group in Poona and there he plotted to kill the governor at a racecourse function. An intelligence agent, Sharat Keshdar, joined their group, Rajguru was arrested due to his betrayal and their conspiracy to kill the governor of the racecourse failed.

Shivaram Rajguru was brought to Lahore, tried for the murder of Saunders and the 'Lahore Conspiracy Case', and sentenced to death. He appeared on the gallows on 23 March 1931, smiling.

Sukhdev Thapar

Sukhdev Thapar was born on May 15, 1908 in Ludhiana, Punjab. Since childhood, he witnessed the oppression of British rule in India and that is why he broke the chain of slavery and joined the revolutionary party. Sukhdev's father's name was Shri Ramlal Thapar, a famous social worker. His father died two years after Sukhdev's birth. Sukhdev was raised by his uncle Shri Achintaram Thapar. At the time of Sukhdev's birth, his uncle Achintaram was serving a sentence in jail. Sukhdev grew up in such a revolutionary atmosphere.

When Sukhdev was a student of the third standard, the Governor came to his school. On the orders of the headmaster, all the students saluted the Governor, but Sukhdev did not do so. Then Sukhdev was asked why he did not salute the Governor, Sukhdev clearly said that he would not salute any Britisher.

Later, Sukhdev and Bhagat Singh started working for the revolutionary party together. They rented a house. They would stay out during the day and return at night. This made the owner of the house and the people around suspicious. Because of this,

Sukhdev brought his mother to that house. Now if anyone asked him anything, would he answer? He was working, there was road work going on far away. He worked day and night and came home late.

Sukhdev was very brave. When bomb-making started in Lahore, he used to bring all the bomb materials from Ferozepur. Once, while going to get materials to make bombs, he mistakenly went to the soldiers' hangout. Because of this, Sukdev had to be beaten a lot. Sukdev was beaten silently, but he didn't say anything, because he had a pistol, cartridges, and bomb-making materials in his pocket. A sepoy asked, "What's in this bag?" Sukdev used his wit and smiled, "Sepoy Ji, there's a pistol and cartridges." The sepoys also laughed and the conversation changed.

When Lala Lajpat Rai died in a lathi charge while opposing the Simon Commission, the revolutionaries who killed Saunders included Sukhdev. This incident shook the British Empire and the revolutionaries and the whole country rejoiced that day. The 'Lahore Conspiracy' case was started after the murder of Saunders. In this case, Shivram Rajguru, Sukhdev and Bhagat Singh were sentenced to death. On 23 March 1931, the revolutionaries appeared on the gallows and created a new urge for freedom in the hearts of the youth of the country. Sukhdev was only 24 years old at the time of his execution.

Bhagwati Charan Vohra

Bhagwati Charan Vohra was born on 4 July 1903 in Agra, Uttar Pradesh. His father Raisaheb Pandit Shiv Charan Lal was a railway worker. Bhagwati Charan studied at the National College, Lahore. The revolutionary fire girl Durgavati Devi (Durga Bhabhi) was Bhagwati Charan's wife. Bhagwati Charan was attracted to patriotism while in college. His classmates during college were Bhagat Singh and Sukhdev Thapar. Bhagwati Charan passed his M.A. from D.A.V. College, Lahore.

Since childhood, he had a strong passion for patriotism, so in 1926 he joined the revolutionary organization 'Bharat Naujawan Sabha'. Once, after hearing that his father Shivcharan Lal was going to receive the title of 'Rai Bahadur' from the British, Bhagwati Charan left home without informing anyone. Then he joined the 'Hindustan Republican Association' and participated in many important revolutionary activities.

On 30th October 1928, at the call of Lala Lajpat Rai, revolutionaries Bhagat Singh, Sukhdev, Bhagwati Charan and other revolutionaries raised slogans against the Simon Commission, 'Simon Go Bag'. There, Lala Lajpat Rai was lathicharged. Lala Lajpat Rai died 17 days later from his injuries. In retaliation, the revolutionaries shot Saunders while trying to kill the police Adhikari Scort. The revolutionaries managed to escape. Bhagwati Charan was actively involved in this massacre along with Bhagat Singh, Rajguru, Sukhdev, and Chandrashekhar Azad.

On 8 April 1929, the police arrested Bhagat Singh, Batukeshwar Dutt and his associates for throwing bombs at the Central Parliament House in Delhi. Then on 23 December 1929, Bhagwati Charan and a revolutionary named Yashpal tried to blow up the Viceroy's special train. An arrest warrant was issued against Bhagwati Charan due to his involvement in various activities of the revolutionaries. Despite many attempts, the police were never able to trace him. The police announced a huge reward in his name, but it was not possible to arrest him.

The revolutionaries then decided that Bhagat Singh, Rajguru, Sukhdev and other revolutionaries should be released from Lahore jail. For this, a bomb had to be made, and they made a bomb. On 28 May 1930, Bhagwati Charan and one of his companions went to the banks of the Ravi river to test the bomb. While testing the bomb, Bhagwati Charan exploded in the hands of vohra and Bhagwati Charan was severely injured and died. The immortal revolutionary Bhagwati Charan was lost to the sound of that bomb.

Durgawati Devi (Durga Bhabhi)

Durgawati Devi was born on 7 October 1907 in Allahabad, Uttar Pradesh. She was the wife of revolutionary Bhagwati Charan Vohra, whom she married when she was only 11 years old. After marriage, Durgawati Devi joined her husband in revolutionary work. On 14 December 1928, Saunders was killed instead of Scott. Bhagat Singh, Rajguru, Sukhdev, Chandrashekhar Azad and Durgawati Devi's companion Bhagwati Charan Vohra were involved in this murder.

After the assassination of Saunders, Durgawati Devi smuggled Bhagat Singh and Rajguru from Lahore to Lucknow and kept them in a safe place. Durgawati Devi managed to smuggle Bhagat Singh's wife in the guise of her. She was known to all revolutionaries as Durga Bhabhi. Durgawati's husband Bhagavati Charan made a bomb to free Bhagat Singh from jail, and while testing the bomb, it exploded in Bhagavati Charan's hand. He died on the spot.

After her husband's death, Durgawati devoted herself completely to the work of the revolution. At that time, she ran here and there for various revolutionary activities, her job was to hide the weapons of the revolutionaries and collect secret information. During the trial, a secret meeting of the revolutionaries was called in Lahore, where there was talk of getting Bhagat Singh released. For this, money was needed, so whoever could bring as much as he could to the party fund. For this, a treasury was opened, and Durgawati donated the first amount of 3000 rupees. At that time, this 3000 thousand rupees was worth a lot. She tried to get Bhagat Singh released by selling her ornaments and valuables. She did another thing to get Bhagat Singh released, she tried to kill the Bombay Police Commissioner.

This is how Durgawati worked for the independence of the country. Finally, she went to live in Ghaziabad (Uttar Pradesh). Durgawati Swami supported the incomplete work of Bhagavati Charan throughout her life and chose it as her path. On October 16, 1999, Durgawati Devi, the fire girl of the fire age, breathed her last in Ghaziabad.

Chandrashekhar Azad

Chandrashekhar Azad was born on 23 July 1906 in the village of Dhawra in Jhabua district of Madhya Pradesh. His father's name was Pandit Sitaram Tiwari. At the age of 15, Chandrashekhar joined the Non-Cooperation Movement in 1921 while he was a student at Banaras Central College. As a result of his participation in the movement, he was arrested and sentenced to 15 lashes. This whipping punishment led him to the path of armed revolution.

After his arrest, when he was asked what his name was, Chandrashekhar replied, "My name is Azad." From then on, the name Azad became associated with his name. Then Chandrashekhar Azad met the revolutionary Rajendra Lahiri and Sachindranath Bakshi. From then on, he joined the active revolutionary party. Gradually, Chandrashekhar was seen as a reliable member of the party. Even then, he had a close relationship with the great revolutionary Ramprasad Bismil and participated in various revolutionary activities under his leadership.

On 9 August 1925, he stopped a train a short distance from Kakori station and looted government money. Later, this case became known as the "Kakori Train Robbery". After this incident, he had to go into hiding for a long time to avoid arrest. In 1928, Lala Lajpat Rai was seriously injured in the movement that started when Simon came to India. In revenge, Chandrashekhar Azad killed Saunders on 14 December 1928, along with Bhagat Singh, Rajguru and Jaigopal, while trying to kill Scott.

On April 8, 1929, Bhagat Singh and Batukeshwar Dutt threw a bomb at the Central Parliament House in Delhi. Chandrashekhar Azad also took part in this plan. After that, almost all the members of the "Hindustan Republican Association" were arrested. But the police could never catch Chandrashekhar Azad. Therefore, the government announced a reward of five thousand rupees for his capture. Chandrashekhar Azad used to say - 'My Mauser will not give the enemy a chance to arrest me.'

Chandrashekhar also planned to free Bhagat Singh and his associates from jail, which resulted in the death of Bhagwati Charan Vohra. Chandrashekhar always jumped into various operations in different places. For this reason, his colleagues gave him the name "Quick Silver". The British never dared to confront Azad due to his terrible activities. Already, CID spies were roaming around behind him. The day was 9 AM on February 27, 1931, Azad was talking to his companion Sukhdev Raj in Alfred Park, Allahabad. On the other hand, with the help of spies, the news reached the British camp. Armed police forces appeared around the park. Azad saw the armed police approaching him with their sights set on him. Azad took out the Mauser pistol from his pocket and took it in his hand. Immediately after that, an armed clash began, with Chandrashekhar Azad alone on one side and the entire police force on the other.

Azad tells Sukhdev Raj to flee the scene, as he will have to lead the next revolution. Alfred Park seems to be shaking at the sound of gunfire. A bullet came and injured Azad. Azad's bullets killed several people, including S.P. Jannat Babar and Thakur Bishweshwar Singh. In the end, only one bullet remained, so he kept that bullet for himself instead of fighting any longer.

Azad thought it best to surrender rather than be captured by the British. So in the end, he put the pistol to his forehead and pulled the trigger, and Azad's life was extinguished in an instant. He fought alone from behind a neem tree and completely destroyed the enemy. Since Azad had been silent for a long time, the British tried to get close to him and repeatedly fired at the dead Azad.

Azad remained Azad in the end, he rightly said he was Azad (independent) and would always remain Azad.

Pandit Kishori Lal

Pandit Kishori Lal was born on 6 June 1909 in the village of Dharmapur in Hoshiarpur district of Punjab. His father's name was Raghubir Dutt Shastri. Raghubir was a professor and was associated with Bhagat Singh's uncle Sardar Ajit Singh in the movement. His elder brother was a social worker and was acquainted with many revolutionaries, due to which Keshorilal came in contact with Bhagat Singh's revolutionary party.

While studying at D.A.B. College Lahore, Keshorilal came in contact with the 'Bharat Naujawan Sabha' and from there Kishori Lal started walking on the path of revolution. Kishori Lal always had a smile on his face. He devoted himself completely to the work of making bombs. He was arrested on April 15, 1929 in the "Lahore Conspiracy Case" in the bomb-making factory of the revolutionaries.

Pandit Keshorilal was sentenced to life imprisonment in the trial for the murder of Saunders and the "Lahore Conspiracy Case". Kishori Lal was acquitted of the death sentence due to his young age. Bhagat Singh, Sukhdev and Shivram Rajguru were sentenced to death in this case. While in Lahore Central Jail, he joined the revolutionaries' hunger strike there. After that, he was sent to various jails.

Finally, he was sent to the Andaman Cellular Jail and started a hunger strike there too. As a result, his companion Mahavir Singh died while on a hunger strike. He spent 17 years in prison. He was released on 21 February 1946. On that day, his friends Gaya Prasad Katiya, Shiv Verma and Jaydev Kapoor were released and they also spent 17 years in prison.

Long after independence, he was seriously injured in a road accident and was admitted to the Civil Hospital. Keshori lal fought for 11 days and breathed his last on 11 July 1990.

Dr. Gaya Prasad Katiyar

Gaya Prasad Katiyar was born on June 20, 1900 in Kanpur, Uttar Pradesh. Gaya Prasad participated in the Non-Cooperation Movement of 1921. Later he joined the "Hindustan Socialist Republican Association". Thus Gaya Prasad joined the armed revolutionary group of the great revolutionary leader Chandrashekhar Azad and another great revolutionary Sardar

Bhagat Singh.

He organized the conspiracy to assassinate Saunders, Sardar Bhagat Singh's central office. Later, Gaya Prasad actively participated in the activities of the revolutionaries, including throwing bombs on the Parliament in Delhi, making bombs, etc. A few days later, Gaya Prasad was arrested while working in the bomb factory in Saharanpur. Gaya Prasad was sentenced to life imprisonment on 7 October 1930 in the trial.

Gaya Prasad was kept in Lahore Jail. While imprisoned in Lahore Jail, he started a hunger strike along with other revolutionary prisoners due to the mistreatment of the jail authorities. He observed a hunger strike for 63 days. Later, Gaya Prasad was sent to Andaman Cellular Jail in Kalapani. Gaya Prasad also started a hunger strike in Andaman Cellular Jail. There too, he remained on a hunger strike for 46 days. Gaya Prasad endured many humiliations and various pains during his entire 17 years in prison. On February 21, 1946, Gaya Prasad was released unconditionally. In 1947, India gained independence, but even in independent India, he had to go to jail due to the struggle for the oppressed people.

Later, the revolutionary Gaya Prasad breathed his last on February 10, 1993.

Vijay Kumar Singh

Vijay Kumar Singh was born on 17 January 1909 in a Bengali family. His father's name was Markand Singh and his mother's name was Sarat Kumari. In 1921, Vijay Kumar participated in the Non-Cooperation Movement, but was saddened when the movement was suddenly stopped. In 1924, he became involved with Bhagat Singh. Vijay Kumar was one of the first in the bomb-making ranks of the revolutionary party "Hindustan Socialist Republican Association", which started in Calcutta under the leadership of Jatin Das.

On 8 April 1929, Bhagat Singh and Batukeshwar Dutt were arrested, and on 15 April the rest of the revolutionaries were arrested, and Vijay Kumar was arrested in Bareilly. In Lahore jail, revolutionary Jatin Das, along with Bhagat Singh and other revolutionaries, began a hunger strike. When revolutionary Jatin Das was counting his last hours after 63 days of hunger strike, he asked his companions to sing a song. Vijay Kumar sang the song 'Ekla Chalo Re' sung by the world poet Rabindranath Tagore.

Vijay Kumar was sentenced to life imprisonment in the ' Saunders murder' and the second 'Lahore conspiracy case', along with his involvement in the bomb case. He was then sent to the Andaman Cellular Jail, where he also went on a hunger strike, which resulted in the death of his companion Mahavir Singh. He was released from the Andaman Cellular Jail in 1938. Later, he was arrested again and imprisoned from 1941-45. He spent a total of 17 years in prison. He finally died on 16 July 1992 in Patna, Bihar.

Shiv Varma

The great revolutionary Shiv Varma was born on 9th February 1907 in Hardoi district of Uttar Pradesh. After participating in the Non-Cooperation Movement, he moved to Kanpur. Shiv Varma met great revolutionaries like Bhagat Singh and Chandrashekhar Azad as a student of D.A.V. College. He joined the "Hindustan Socialist Republican Association" as an active member. Then he played a key role in this organization in Kanpur.

A day before the hanging of revolutionary Ramprasad Bismil in the "Kakori Kand Case", Shiv Verma met him in Gorakhpur Jail in the guise of his brother. After that, Shiv Verma got involved in various revolutionary activities. He was involved in the "Saunders murder", the second "Lahore conspiracy case" and the bomb case in the Central Parliament House in Delhi. After this incident, when the arrests began, he was arrested on 15 April 1929 along with other revolutionaries.

When the trial began, he was sentenced to life imprisonment in the "Lahore conspiracy case" and the "Saunders murder case". Finally, the great revolutionary Shiv Verma died in Kanpur on 10

January 1997.

Dhanvantari

Dhanvantari was born on 7 March 1902 in Jammu. Father Durga Dutt Mahe. Dhambantari passed his matriculation from Jammu S.R. School and joined Lahore College to study Ayurveda. During his studies, he joined the "Hindustan Socialist Republican Association." He soon developed a good relationship with Bhagat Singh. He was arrested by the police from a bomb-making factory in the 'Lahore Conspiracy Case'.

He was convicted of treason in the ' Saunders murder case' and the 'Delhi conspiracy case'. Then the revolutionaries protested against the infamous Cellular Jail for keeping political prisoners in the same cell with other prisoners. He began a hunger strike, and the revolutionary Dhanvantari went on a hunger strike for a total of 61 days. He was then released in 1939. The revolutionary Dhambanthari died on 13 July 1953 at the age of 51.

Prem Dutt Varma

Prem Dutt Varma was born on 19 September 1911. Prem Dutt Varma was arrested on charges of involvement in the "Saunders Murder" case. He was a member of the "Hindustan Socialist Republican Association". During the trial, cases were filed in the court against Bhagat Singh, Rajguru, Jatin Das and Prem Dutt Varma and other revolutionaries. Among the revolutionaries, Jaigopal became a witness for the government. Jaigopal was one of the conspirators in the Saunders murder case.

Jaigopal became a witness to save his life, when he testified against the revolutionaries in court, Prem Dutt Varma took off his shoe and hit Jaigopal in the face. Then, in court, each of the revolutionaries was forcibly handcuffed. The trial resulted in the death sentence of Bhagat Singh, Rajguru and Sukhdev. The revolutionaries were sentenced to various terms due to Jaigopal's betrayal.

Prem dutt Verma was sentenced to 3 years of rigorous imprisonment due to his young age and he also said in court, "If you let the traitor Jaygopal get hit with one more shoe, then I am willing to serve a few more years of sentence."

Sushila Mohan (Didi)

Sushila Mohan was born on 5 March 1905 in present-day Pakistan. In Dehradun, she met revolutionary Bhagat Singh and other revolutionaries. All the revolutionaries called her Didi. After the assassination of Saunders, Bhagat Singh moved from Lahore to Kolkata with the help of Durgavati Devi. Bhagat Singh and other revolutionaries took shelter with Sushila Mohan in Kolkata. Sushila Mohan Didi, along with Bhagavathi Charan and Yashpal, conspired to blow up the Viceroy's special train with a bomb.

Sushila Mohan participated in various activities of the revolutionaries. Sushila Didi's job was to hide weapons and send weapons to other places. Apart from this, she participated in the 'Quit India' movement. Didi used to propagate the revolution among women. Finally, this fire girl breathed her last on January 13, 1963.

THE END